John Fletcher

Twayne's English Authors Series

Arthur F. Kinney, Editor

University of Massachusetts, Amherst

TEAS 433

JOHN FLETCHER
(1579–1625)
From the collection of the Earl of Clarendon
and reproduced by his permission

John Fletcher

By Charles L. Squier

University of Colorado–Boulder

Twayne Publishers
A Division of G.K. Hall & Co. • Boston

John Fletcher

Charles L. Squier

Copyright © 1986 by G.K. Hall & Co.
All Rights Reserved
Published by Twayne Publishers
A Division of G.K. Hall & Co.
70 Lincoln Street
Boston, Massachusetts 02111

Copyediting supervised by Lewis DeSimone
Book production by Elizabeth Todesco
Book design by Barbara Anderson

Typeset in 11 pt. Garamond
by Modern Graphics, Inc., Weymouth, Massachusetts

Printed on permanent/durable acid-free paper
and bound in the United States of America

Library of Congress Cataloging in Publication Data

Squier, Charles L.
  John Fletcher.

  (Twayne's English authors series; TEAS 433)
  Bibliography: p. 162
  Includes indexes.
  1. Fletcher, John, 1579–1625—Criticism and
interpretation. I. Title. II. Series.
PR2514.S68 1986   822'.3   86–12136
ISBN 0–8057–6923–4

For Jan

Contents

Editor's Note

For some time we have only thought of John Fletcher in connection with others—as the collaborator with Francis Beaumont or, more importantly, with Shakespeare whom he succeeded as chief playwright for the King's Men and the boys' company at Blackfriars—or as the founder of English tragicomedy. Charles L. Squier persuasively argues a different view: that on his own, Fletcher was the most popular playwright of his age (and indirectly founded the Restoration comedy of manners that followed him) because he was essentially theatrical and commercial. By examining in detail a large number of plays by Fletcher alone and with others, Squier shows that Fletcher's recipe for success was a kind of *olla podrida,* a mixed stew of ingredients such as comedy, satire, and romance, from which emerged a drama of paradox grounded in "the rhetoric of the improbable." Unlikely situations, exaggerated gestures, stylization through plot and witty conceit, per- verse awareness of the comic consciousness, and unabashed theatricality that calls attention largely to itself, its own fictionality—a kind of metatheatrics—were all part of Fletcher's unique and widely successful art. As Squier notes, "Fletcher's comic world is varied in tone, in dramatic types, in characters, and in the range of comic language. Romance and tragicomedy mix easily with comedy of wit, satire, farce, and bawdy horseplay. Grotesques leer out from dark corners and varities of clowns dance and cavort in sunny meadows and beery taverns. The range and strength of his comic language is remarkable and extends far beyond the witty exchange of gentlemen on their way to the comedy of manners of the Restoration. If there is not a coherent comic vision, there is a sure sense of human folly and absurdity; and there is a plenitude of surprise and laughter, a superb sense of comic timing, of the structures of action and language that make up the comic moment." Long thought of as the man who introduced tragicomedy from the Italian stage to the English, Fletcher is seen here instead as one who used the forms, possibilities, and techniques inherent in tragicomedy to write even more important comedy that took center stage throughout the seventeenth century in England.

—Arthur F. Kinney

About the Author

Charles L. Squier took his undergraduate training at Harvard, to which he returned after military service for an M.A.T. He received a Ph.D. in English from the University of Michigan. Since 1963 he has taught at the University of Colorado—Boulder, where he is a professor of English. In 1974–75 he was an exchange professor at the University of Liverpool and in 1981–82 he taught at the Tianjin Foreign Languages Institute, Tianjin, People's Republic of China. He coedited *The Sonnet* and is the author of *Sir John Suckling* in this series. His publications also include poetry and short fiction.

Preface

John Fletcher succeeded Shakespeare as the chief playwright for the King's Men and became one of the most popular and prolific playwrights of the seventeenth century. At the time of his death in 1625 he was considered equal and sometimes superior to the greatest writers for the stage of the century, William Shakespeare and Ben Jonson. His popularity and reputation continued unabated for a half-century after his death. The tragicomic style that he and his sometime collaborator Francis Beaumont perfected dominated the stage for as many years.

Although plays in the Fletcher canon are now seldom produced, his work remains of great interest to students of seventeenth-century drama. He bridges the years between Shakespeare and Dryden and illuminates their shifting tastes, techniques, and concerns. His stage language, with its clarity and directness, appealed strongly to the Restoration.

The plays, moreover, retain more than just an historical literary interest. A few of the plays are still acted with some frequency and an occasional play is presented in revised and refurbished form. More are worth reviving; that they are not is a loss to theater audiences. The reader of the plays can still find pleasure in the texts, thus joining such illustrious dead as Samuel Taylor Coleridge, who read, enjoyed, and commented extensively on Fletcher; Herman Melville, who quoted him in his works; and Henry James, who whiled away hours in his London club reading Fletcher. Anyone, moreover, interested in the craft of dramatic writing can look to Fletcher as to one of the mastercraftsmen and entertainers of the English stage.

Fletcher wrote, alone or in collaboration, over fifty plays. This study makes no attempt to discuss or even mention each and every play, but concentrates on selected plays from each of the major dramatic genres. His collaboration with Shakespeare is given only passing mention since it, and the works involved, have been discussed extensively elsewhere and more particularly in the Shakespearean canon. The first chapter is devoted to Fletcher's life and a quick survey of his theatrical work. The next three chapters discuss, first, the early collaborative plays and those written for the children's acting troops; next, a chapter each is devoted to tragicomedy, tragedy, and comedy. The final chapter considers Fletcher's reputation and achievement.

I wish to thank my colleagues John L. Murphy, John M. Major, and R. L. Saner for helpful advice. My wife gave me consistent encouragement and my children and their friends listened to lengthy plot summaries. For such forebearance I am grateful.

Quotations from *The Dramatic Works in the Beaumont and Fletcher Canon* are printed with permission of Cambridge University Press. The anonymously painted portrait of John Fletcher is reproduced from the collection of the earl of Clarendon with his kind permission.

Charles L. Squier

University of Colorado—Boulder

A Note on the Texts

The most recent and best edition of Fletcher, *The Dramatic Works in the Beaumont and Fletcher Canon*, general editor Fredson Bowers (Cambridge, 1966–), is not yet complete. Quotations are taken from this edition whenever possible. Otherwise I have used *The Works of Beaumont and Fletcher*, edited by Arnold Glover and A. R. Waller (Cambridge, 1905–12). In a few instances quotations are taken from the folio *Comedies and Tragedies Written by Francis Beaumont and John Fletcher Gentlemen* (London, 1647). The text used for a particular play is indicated in parenthesis by an abbreviation for the edition and a volume number after the first quotation. Since line numbers are not given in Glover and Waller, citations throughout are by act, scene, and page. The following abbreviations are used in citations:

Folio *Comedies and Tragedies Written by Francis Beaumont and John Fletcher Gentlemen* (London, 1647)

  DW *The Dramatic Works in the Beaumont and Fletcher Canon*, general editor Fredson Bowers, 5 vols. (Cambridge, 1966–82)

    W *The Works of Beaumont and Fletcher*, edited by Arnold Glover and A. R. Waller, 10 vols. (Cambridge, 1905–12)

After the initial citation the *DW* or *W* indication is dropped.

Chronology

1579   John Fletcher is born in Rye, Sussex, and baptized on 20 December.

1591   Admitted pensioner to Bene't College (Corpus Christi), Cambridge.

1592   Mother dies.

1594   Father, Richard Fletcher, having held the bishoprics of Bristol and Worcester, is elected bishop of London.

1595   Bishop Fletcher remarries and loses the favor of Queen Elizabeth.

1596   Father dies.

1606   Writes plays for the boy companies and the private theaters and begins collaboration with Francis Beaumont. *The Woman Hater* performed.

1607   *The Knight of the Burning Pestle* and *Cupid's Revenge* performed; *The Woman Hater* published.

1608   *The Faithful Shepherdess* performed.

1609   Undated quarto of *The Faithful Shepherdess* published about this time with commendatory verses by Ben Jonson. *The Coxcomb* performed.

1610   The King's Men begin acting at Blackfriars' Theater and Fletcher and Beaumont write for them. *Philaster, Wit at Several Weapons* performed.

1611   *The Maid's Tragedy, A King and No King, The Night Walker,* and *The Woman's Prize* performed.

1612   Beaumont marries and retires from playwriting about this time. *The Captain* performed.

1613   Fletcher and Shakespeare collaborate on *The Two Noble Kinsmen* and *Henry VIII. Four Plays, or Moral Representations in One; Bonduca, The Scornful Lady,* and *The Honest Man's Fortune* are acted.

1614   *Valentinian* and *Wit Without Money* staged.

1615   *Cupid's Revenge* is published.

1616   Francis Beaumont dies in March and William Shakespeare in April. Fletcher becomes the chief playwright for the King's Men. *The Scornful Lady* is published. *Monsieur Thomas, Love's Pilgrimage,* and *The Nice Valour* are performed.

1617   *The Mad Lover* and *The Queen of Corinth* are performed.

1618   *Thierry and Theodoret* and *The Loyal Subject* are acted.

1619   *The Maid's Tragedy* and *A King and No King* are published. *The Humorous Lieutenant, The Bloody Brother (Rollo, Duke of Normandy),* and *Sir John van Olden Barnavelt* are staged.

1620   *Philaster* is published. *The Little French Lawyer, The Laws of Candy, Women Pleased, The Custom of the Country,* and *The Double Marriage* are performed.

1621   *Thierry and Theodoret* is published. *The False One, The Island Princess, The Wild Goose Chase,* and *Beggars' Bush* are performed.

1622   *The Prophetess, The Sea Voyage,* and *The Spanish Curate* are acted.

1623   *The Wandering Lovers* and *The Maid in the Mill* are performed.

1624   *Rule a Wife and Have a Wife, A Wife for a Month, The Chances,* and *The Elder Brother* are performed.

1625   *The Noble Gentleman* and *The Fair Maid of the Inn* are acted. John Fletcher dies of the plague in August.

1647   *Comedies and Tragedies Written by Francis Beaumont and John Fletcher.*

1679   *Fifty Comedies and Tragedies.*

Chapter One

Master John Fletcher, Playwright: The Life

Beaumont and Fletcher: "Renowned Twinnes of Poetry"

In 1647 the Royalist cause was as good as lost; only a few scenes remained before the tragedy ended with the execution of King Charles I on the scaffold before Whitehall on 30 January 1649. The darkness of the times was compounded, at least for those who had patronized the lively and thriving theaters of London, by the silence of those theaters, closed now for five years by the Puritan opponents of the stage. Clearly there was little hope for the resumption of regular playing. Theatergoers, then, must have welcomed with a poignant enthusiasm the publication in folio of *Comedies and Tragedies Written by Francis Beaumont And John Fletcher Gentlemen: Never printed before, And now published by the Authours Originall Copies.*

This volume, a joint venture by two publishers, Humphrey Robinson and Humphrey Moseley, supplied readers with thirty-four plays and a masque. Some of the plays were indeed the collaborations of Beaumont and Fletcher; many were the work of John Fletcher alone; and others were Fletcher's collaborations with other dramatists, including Nathan Field, William Rowley, and, above all, Philip Massinger. A more accurate title might have been "The Plays of John Fletcher, Written Alone and in Collaboration for the King's Men," but such accuracy would not sell as well as the linked names of Beaumont and Fletcher.

The publication of the folio was clearly a major literary event. The work was divided among several printing houses, and in "The Stationer to the Reader" Humphrey Moseley asserts the care and expense that went into publication:

Twere vaine to mention the *Chargeablenesse* of the Work; for those who own'd the *Manuscripts,* too well knew their value to make a cheap estimate of any of these Pieces, and though another joyn'd with me in the *Purchase* and Printing, yet the *Care & Pains* was wholly mine, which I found to be more than you'l easily imagine, unlesse you knew into how many hands the Originalls were dispersed. They are all now happily met in this Book, having escaped these *Publike Troubles,* free and unmangled. Heretofore when Gentlemen desired but a Copy of any of these *Playes,* the meanest piece here (if any may be called Meane where every one is Best) cost them more then foure times the price you pay for the whole Volume.[1]

The plays were purchased from the surviving members of the King's Men (and presumably from other sources) who signed the dedication to the volume to the earl of Pembroke. While the theaters were open the players guarded their dramatic property; with the theaters closed the plays could at least provide ready cash for unemployed actors. Moseley may have had in mind a speculation beyond publication, based on the hope that the theaters would eventually reopen, for in 1660 he claimed that he owned the acting rights to the plays he had published in the folio.

A further measure of the importance of the publication of the folio is evident when one recalls that only two other playwrights received folio publication in the seventeenth century, William Shakespeare and Ben Jonson. It is in this high company that the collective entity of Beaumont and Fletcher was placed by critical opinion of the age, a reputation that remained undiminished until almost the end of the century.

One expects the prefatory matter of a work such as this to be filled with high praise and puffery, and the tributes in the 1647 folio do not disappoint. The contributors, including Richard Lovelace, Edmund Waller, John Denham, Richard Brome, and Robert Herrick, constitute a veritable roll call of Cavalier poets, dramatists, and literati. Succeeding Fletcher's collaborator Philip Massinger as chief dramatist for the King's Men, James Shirley has pride of place in his witty and hyperbolical address "To the Reader"; only to mention Beaumont and Fletcher, he writes, "is to throw a cloude upon all former names and benight posterity" (Folio, A3v).

Although "Beaumont and Fletcher" were linked together by the title of the folio and by their latter-day seventeenth-century reputation as, to cite Thomas Fuller's representative epithet, twin stars "like Castor and pollux (most happy when in conjunction) [who] raised the English to equal the Athenian and Roman Theater: Beaumont bringing the *ballast* of judgement, Fletcher the *sail* of phantasie; both compounding a poet to admiration,"[2] the reality of the limits of the collaboration is recognized by the fact that of thirty-seven commentatory poems twenty-five are directed to Fletcher alone. Jasper Mayne's declaration in his tribute to the "Great paire of *Authors* . . . / . . . both so knit, / That no man knowes where to divide your wit" (Folio, d) reflects real difficulties in determining precise details of the Beaumont-Fletcher collaboration, but needs to be qualified by the knowledge that it had begun by 1606, perhaps as early as 1604, and ended in 1612 or 1613 with Beaumont's marriage and retirement to the country. But Fletcher continued to write until his death in 1625, and his plays make up the bulk of the 1647 folio.

The collaboration served, however, to establish the future myth of a compound playwright called "Beaumont and Fletcher," "Renowned Twinnes of Poetry" (Folio, f3), as Alexander Brome puts it, a myth aided and abetted by John Aubrey's delightful but unreliable biographical assertion that "They lived together on the Banke side, not far from the Play-house, both batchelors; lay together; had one wench in the house between them, which they did so admire; the same cloathes and cloak, &c.; between them."[3] Sir John Birkenhead's description of "two Voyces in one song . . . / (*Fletcher's* keen *Trebble,* and deep *Beaumont's* Base)" (Folio, E, v) is, then, more a poetic fiction than a reality, but a description of the life of Francis Beaumont is appropriate and pertinent to the beginnings of John Fletcher's dramatic career.

Francis Beaumont

Francis Beaumont was born in 1583 or 1584, the third son of Francis Beaumont, justice of the Court of Common Pleas, at the manor of Grace Dieu in Leicestershire. His grandfather, John Beaumont, had obtained the nunnery of Grace Dieu in the reign of Henry VIII. Francis Beaumont's father was a prosperous land owner and the family connections comprised a master roll of some of the greatest names of English aristocracy. The three sons, Henry, John, and Francis, entered Broadgates Hall (now Pembroke College), Oxford, in 1597. Francis left without taking a degree and was admitted to Inner Temple, one of the four Inns of Court, where young gentlemen studied law and entertained themselves with poetry, gambling, drinking, wenching, playgoing, and other pursuits. While there,

Beaumont contributed a mock grammatical lecture to a Christmas revel, but his literary career may well have begun with the anonymous publication of an Ovidian narrative poem, *Salmacis and Hermaphroditus* (1602).[4] In the same year his brother John began his poetic career with the publication of the mock-heroic *The Metamorphosis of Tobacco*.

In the eighth eclogue of a revision of *Idea, the Shepherd's Garland* in *Poems Lyrick and Pastoral* (1606), Michael Drayton celebrates in pastoral guise his friendship with the Beaumont family at Grace Dieu: the sister Elizabeth as well as John and Francis:

> Then that dear nymph that in the Muses joys,
> That in wild Charnwood with her flocks doth go,
> Mirtilla, sister to those hopeful boys,
> My loved Thyrsis and sweet Palmeo;
>   That oft to Soar the southern shepherds bring,
>   Of whose clear waters they divinely sing.[5]

Sir John Beaumont retains a minor place in the history of the heroic couplet. Francis Beaumont's more substantial literary position and link with the great figures of the London theatrical world is evidenced in Ben Jonson's laudatory epigram 55 which begins, "How do I love thee *Beaumont* and thy Muse"[6] (praise to be qualified by Jonson's remark to William Drummond that "Francis Beaumont loved too much himself and his own verse").[7] "Mr. Francis Beaumont's letter to Ben Jonson" celebrates their friendship and the witty comaraderie of literary circles of London with its often quoted lines:

> What things have we seen
> Done at the Mermaid! heard words that have been
> So nimble and so full of subtill flame,
> As if that every one from whence they came,
> Had meant to put his whole wit in a jest,
> And had resolv'd to live a foole the rest
> Of his dull life; then when there hath been throwne
> Wit able enough to justifie the Towne
> For three dayes past, wit that might warrant be
> For the whole City to talke foolishly
> Till that were cancel'd, and when that was gone,
> We left an aire behind us, which alone,

Was able to make the two next companies
Right witty; though but downright fools, more wise.
(Folio, sec. 3 [p. 167])

Beaumont's contribution to the dramatic portion of that literary world begins with his collaboration with John Fletcher on *The Woman Hater* (1606), a comedy in the manner of Jonson and Chapman written for the boys' company, the Children of Paul's. Beaumont was the major contributor to *The Woman Hater*. It was published in quarto in 1607, and in the same year Beaumont's *The Knight of the Burning Pestle* was presented by the Children of the Queen's Revels. This play, entirely or almost entirely written by Beaumont, is undoubtedly the most popular and enduring of all the "Beaumont and Fletcher" plays, the only play in the canon still to be acted regularly. The comedy was, however, a failure when first produced.

The Children of the Revels were also the performers of the next collaborative work, *Cupid's Revenge,* acted somewhere between 1607 and 1612.[8] Still another collaborative work for the Children of the Revels was *The Coxcomb* (1608–10). *Philaster* (1608–10), a tragicomedy written for the King's Men, the adult company playing both at the Globe and at Blackfriars Theater for which William Shakespeare was still the chief author, was the collaborators' first success, an unqualified hit of which the greater share is attributed to Beaumont. *The Maid's Tragedy* (1608–11), again for the King's Men and again successful, is also attributed largely to Beaumont. Of the third popular tragicomedy, *A King and No King* (1611), Fletcher seems to have written the greater share. Fletcher's contribution also appears to dominate in *The Scornful Lady* (1613–16), although Beaumont may have been responsible for the revision of this comedy acted by the Children of the Revels. Beaumont's contribution to *The Captain* (1609–12), a comedy also likely to have been written for one of the boys' companies, is still less clear.

Some time around 1612 or 1613 Beaumont married an heiress, Ursula Isley of Sundridge, Kent, and apparently retired to the country; at any rate, his career as a writer for the theater ended. The last dramatic piece to be mentioned, his alone, is *The Masque of the Inner Temple and Gray's Inn,* a lavish spectacle performed on 20 February 1613 as part of the series of courtly entertainments in honor of the marriage of King James's daughter, Princess Elizabeth, to Frederick, the Elector Palitinate. Beaumont did not live long after retirement. He died in 1616 and was buried in Westminster Abbey.

John Fletcher

John Fletcher became, in succession to William Shakespeare, the major dramatist for the leading company of London, the King's Men, but beyond the record of his plays the details of his life are scanty. If his connections were not as aristocratic as those of Francis Beaumont, they were sufficiently genteel. His father, Richard, was an ambitious and successful cleric who was in turn dean of Peterborough, bishop of Bristol, bishop of Worcester, and bishop of London as well as chaplain to the queen. As dean of Peterborough it was Richard Fletcher who at the execution of Mary, Queen of Scots, at Fotheringay "knelt down on the scaffold steps and started to pray out loud and at length, in a prolonged and rhetorical style as though determined to force his way into the pages of history" and who cried out at her death, "So perish all the Queen's enemies!"[9] John Fletcher was eight at the time, having been born in 1579 in Rye, Sussex, his father then the minister of Rye. He was the second son and the fourth of nine children.

John Fletcher is not an unusual name in the registers of Oxford and Cambridge of the period, but since his father had been president of Bene't College (Corpus Christi), Cambridge, it is most likely that he is the " 'John Fletcher of London,' who was admitted pensioner to Bene't College on 15 October 1591."[10] It is less certain, but possible, that he might have been the John Fletcher granted a B.A. in 1594/95 and an A.M. in 1598. His father was made bishop of London in 1594/95, no doubt providing young John with an elevated entrance to London life and society; these episcopal advantages, however, were short-lived, ended by his father's remarriage and death in rapid succession. John Fletcher's mother had died in 1592. In 1595 Bishop Fletcher chose to marry Maria, the newly widowed wife of Sir Richard Baker of Sissinghurst, Kent. This marriage cost him the favor of the queen "(who hardly held the second matches of Bishops excusable), accounted his marriage a trespasse on his gravity, whereupon he fell into her deep displeasure. Hereof this Bishop was sadly sensible, and seeking to lose his sorrow in a mist of smoak, died of the immoderate taking thereof, June the 15th, 1596."[11] At that time, as Gayley suggests, young John may have come under the protection of his Uncle Giles Fletcher, who petitioned the queen to show commiseration on the bishop's children, pointing out that " 'He hath left behind him 8 poore children, whereof divers are very young. His dettes due to the Quenes Majestie and to other creditors are 1400*li* or thereaboutes, his whole state is but one house wherein the widow claimeth her thirds, his plate valewed at 400*li*, his other stuffe at 500*li*."[12] The earl of Essex joined in the plea for assistance, but the results are unknown. G. E. Bentley offers the possibility that Fletcher's connection with the earl of Huntingdon began at this time, quoting Philip Massinger's "Copie of a Letter . . ." written sometime after 1615 to the earl of Pembroke:

> I know
> That Iohnson much of what he has does owe
> To you and to your familie, and is neuer
> Slow to professe it, nor had Fletcher euer
> Such Reputation, and credit wonne
> But by his honord Patron, Huntington.[13]

Additional evidence of the Huntingdon connection is Fletcher's own verse letter to the countess of Huntingdon in which he wishes he were at the Huntingdon great house at Ashby:

> There I am sure
> I should have Brawne, and Brackett, wch indure
> Longer then twentie Tryumphs; and good Swan,
> able to choake Th'ambition of a churchman,
> and Pyes cum privlegio, without sinne
> forbydding all to make 'um, but Ralph Goodwin. . . .[14]

The references to choice and abundant food are part of the tradition of the great house poem, but also call to mind frequent references to food in the plays. It is tempting to think that the fleer at ambitious churchmen is a youthful gibe at his father, the late bishop of London, but the most that really can be claimed is that the poem confirms the patronage of the earl and countess of Huntingdon.

Fletcher's whereabouts and activities from the time of his father's death until his theatrical career begins remain unknown as does even his marital state. Thomas Shadwell has a character in his play *Bury-*

Fair (1689) declare, "I knew *Fletcher,* my Friend Fletcher, and his Maid *Joan:* Well, I shall never forget him, I have Supp'd with him, at his House, on the *Bankside:* He lov'd a fat Loyn of Pork of all things in the World: and *Joan,* his Maid, had her Beerglass of Sack; and we all kiss'd her, i'faith, and were as merry as pass'd." The lines are the sort based on some oral tradition and no doubt led Fletcher's nineteenth-century editor, Alexander Dyce, to accept a marriage entry for John Fletcher and Joan Herring in 1612 and a baptismal record of " 'John the son of John Fletcher and Joan his wife"[15] in 1619 as referring to the playwright. Bentley is skeptical of both; Fletcher's marriage must remain a question.

The first of the Beaumont and Fletcher collaborations, as we have seen, was *The Woman Hater,* acted in 1606 and published in 1607. Fletcher's first independent work was *The Faithful Shepherdess,* a pastoral play written for the Children of the Queen's Revels and acted in 1608 or 1609 and published around 1609. This play was a failure, but its publication was accompanied by commendatory poems by Ben Jonson (for whose *Volpone* Fletcher had written commendatory verses, "To the True Master in his Art, B. Jonson" in 1607); Beaumont; the actor and playwright Nathan Field; and the dramatist and translator of Homer, George Chapman. Fletcher was well started on his theatrical career and his biographical record henceforth is the history of his productions as a dramatist.

The Professional Dramatist: An Overview

John Fletcher began writing with Beaumont and by himself for the companies of boy actors which for a time rivaled the adult companies at the Globe, the Fortune, and the other "public" theaters. The children's companies had their origins in choir schools whose masters recognized the commercial possibilities of the choristers as actors. The major companies were the Children of Paul's and the Children of the Chapel Royal, the latter known also as the Children of the Queen's Revels and the Children of Blackfriars. The children's companies sometimes played at court but primarily in what have come to be known as "private" theaters, smaller than the public theaters and roofed, using artificial light, charging a higher admission price, and attracting a more affluent audience than the public theaters.[16]

The differences between the audiences of the private and public theaters have been much debated; it is a debate complicated by the fact that in 1608–9 the King's Men took over Blackfriars as their winter theater while continuing to perform at the Globe in the summer. Although the audiences at the private theaters were somewhat less mixed than those found at the public playhouses, the sophistication of these "coterie" audiences has been overemphasized. Both *The Knight of the Burning Pestle* and *The Faithful Shepherdess* failed initially and both Beaumont and Fletcher attributed the failures to the lack of sophistication of the audiences.

At any rate, Fletcher's dramatic career began with plays written for the private theaters and for the particular conditions and styles of the boy actors: "an eyrie of children, little eyases, that cry out on the top of the question, and are most tyranically clapped for't. These are now the fashion, and so berattle the common stages—so they call them—that many wearing rapiers are afraid of goose-quills and scarce come thither,"[17] as Shakespeare has Rosencrantz describe the children to Hamlet. When the adult actors of the King's Company began playing at Blackfriars, however, Fletcher started to write for them and he continued to do so until his death. Fletcher was not, as was Shakespeare, a shareholder in the company; but from 1609–10 on he apparently wrote exclusively for the King's Men, and after Shakespeare's retirement followed him as the company's chief dramatist. He became one of the eight "regular professionals or attached professionals"[18] who were under contract as writers for the various London theater companies from 1590 to 1642. Bentley lists the eight in order of their dramatic productivity as Thomas Heywood, Fletcher, Thomas Dekker, Massinger, Shakespeare, James Shirley, William Rowley, and Richard Brome.

The attached professionals agreed not to publish their plays without the permission of their company, and only nine of Fletcher's plays were published in his lifetime. Of these, five were written for the children while four belonging to the King's Men show no evidence of authorial cooperation in the printing. Bentley concludes that "the sharers of the King's company were successful in keeping more than 90 percent of his compositions from reaching the hands of the printers by any means—legitimate or illegitimate—during the reign of James I."[19]

Fletcher's industry is impressive. Between 1609 and 1625, Bentley figures, Fletcher was involved in the writing of forty-two plays: "at least 21 of them have been shown to be collaborations including

work of Beaumont, Field, Shakespeare, Rowley, and especially Massinger. If we assume that Fletcher's lines in these collaborations
would have been, on the average, approximately half the play, then
his contribution to the repertory of the King's Men . . . would
have been about 32 plays in a period of 16 years. This is reasonably
close to the norm of two plays a year found in the contracted work
of Brome, Shirley, and Massinger."[20] In addition to furnishing new
plays the professional dramatist was expected to revise old ones and
to write new prologues and epilogues for revivals. Although records
of payment do not exist for the regular dramatists of the King's
Men, the richest of the acting companies, other records show that
dramatists received "very respectable incomes for the time."[21] If
Aubrey's portrait of the impecunious playwright sharing digs and
clothes with Beaumont has any validity, the time of poverty is likely
to have been relatively brief. The portrait of Fletcher in the collection
of the earl of Clarendon (reproduced as the frontispiece to this book)
is certainly that of a confident and prosperous gentleman, dressed
and posed with all the dignity appropriate to his achievements as
dramatist to King James's Men.

Approximate dating makes it difficult to show Fletcher's career
in a firmly chronological, developmental pattern. Collaboration and
revision complicate the matter even more. *The Nice Valour, or the
Passionate Madman,* for example, has been dated between 1615 and
1625, and the play as we have it was probably revised by Thomas
Middleton (or someone else). *The Night Walker, or The Little Thief*
was revised by Shirley in 1633, but was possibly first written and
acted around 1611. These are not atypical examples.

The plays written for the boy actors can be seen as forming a
distinct and discernible grouping. The remainder of the plays in
themes, character, and style present something close to a seamless
whole. That seamlessness is compounded by the very fact of writing
for a repertory company with both specific audiences and actors in
mind. Fletcher, moreover, in his two decades as a professional dramatist, established his own effective dramatic voice, style, and technique. Fletcherian tragicomedy caught the tastes of the times and
dominated the stage of his day and well beyond. It is not entirely
unfair to describe the tragedies in tone and manner as tragicomedies
with deaths. The unity of the comedies is as much as anything in
their disunity or, rather, their variety of types, tones, and styles:
romantic, bawdy, satiric, gulling comedy and knockabout farce. In

the *Essay of Dramatic Poesy* John Dryden, an heir to Fletcher's comedy, admired Fletcher's imitation of "the conversation of gentlemen," the voice that would characterize Restoration comedy, but also loud in Fletcher's comic plays are the voices of ferocious and voracious women and, above all, madmen and eccentrics. A generic division of the plays establishes Fletcher's proportionate interests: twenty-four comedies, sixteen tragicomedies, and eight tragedies plus two "others," *Four Plays, or Moral Representation in One* and *The False One,* a history.

A further division is that of collaborative and independent works. After the collaboration with Beaumont ended, Fletcher's major collaborator, beginning in 1616, was Philip Massinger, born in 1583, the son of Arthur Massinger, a gentleman in the service of Henry Herbert, the second earl of Pembroke. Philip Massinger studied at Oxford but left without a degree, possibly because of a shortage of money after his father's death, and began to earn a sometimes precarious living in the theater as a journeyman playwright-collaborator. The plays he and Fletcher produced together include at the least *The Queen of Corinth, Thierry and Theodoret, The Knight of Malta, The Bloody Brother, The Little French Lawyer, Sir John van Olden Barnavelt, The Custom of the Country, The Double Marriage, The False One, Beggar's Bush, The Prophetess, The Sea Voyage,* and *The Spanish Curate.* Fletcher and Massinger were also good friends, as Sir Aston Cockayne recorded in an epitaph on the playwrights in *A Chaine of Golden Poems* (1658):

> In the same Grave *Fletcher* was buried here
> Lies the Stage-Poet *Philip Massinger:*
> Playes they did write together, were great friends,
> And now one Grave includes them at their ends:
> So whom on earth nothing did part, beneath
> Here (in their Fames) they lie, in spight of death.[22]

But Massinger died in 1640; "one grave" need not be literally taken.

Nathan Field (1587–1620), an actor as well as dramatist, also had a hand in *The Queen of Corinth* and *The Knight of Malta.* Field is likely to have written two of *Four Plays, or Moral Representations in One.* Another actor-dramatist, William Rowley (d. 1626), who specialized in fat clown roles on the stage, certainly contributed to *The Maid in the Mill* and possibly, as with Field, to some other plays as well.

Fletcher's collaboration with Shakespeare has inevitably attracted considerable interest, but does not actually loom large in his career. Only three plays are involved. The lost play *Cardenio* was acted in 1612–13. Humphrey Moseley, the publisher, listed it in 1653 in the Stationers' Register as "The History of Cardenio, by Mr. Fletcher & Shakespeare." It was next heard of when Lewis Theobald, dramatist and editor of Shakespeare, who is forever enthroned as the hero of Alexander Pope's *Dunciad,* presented *The Double Falsehood* at Drury Lane Theater in 1727 and published it in 1728 as a revision of the lost *Cardenio.* Theobald's *The Double Falsehood* remains, but not the manuscript(s) on which it was based. The argument continues as to whether or not Theobald's play is a forgery.

The Two Noble Kinsmen was also acted in 1613. The earliest text of the play, a 1634 quarto, credits Shakespeare and Fletcher as authors. It is not included in the First Folio of Shakespeare's plays, but it is printed in the 1679 second folio of Beaumont and Fletcher. Fletcher's collaboration in *The Two Noble Kinsmen* is certain, but his part in *Henry VIII* is far more questionable.

The Famous History of the Life of King Henry the Eighth was written and acted in 1613 as well. Its performance on 29 June 1613 is especially notable because the cannon fired in the first act set fire to the thatched roof of the Globe, destroying the theater. The argument that Fletcher contributed to *Henry VIII* was advanced in the middle of the nineteenth century using linguistic evidence and has been vigorously debated since. Shakespeare retired to Stratford after 1612. Kenneth Muir's speculation concerning *The Two Noble Kinsmen* might well apply to *Cardenio* and *Henry VIII* as well: "Perhaps Shakespeare, on one of his last visits to London, was prevailed upon to help his old fellows by writing something for the . . . theatre, as they were short of new plays for the forthcoming season. Shakespeare . . . agreed to write as much as he could in the time."[23] Whatever the circumstances of the collaboration, it was limited to the end of Shakespeare's career. But it is just as surely indicative of Fletcher's growing status as playwright for the King's Men.

The plays that Fletcher wrote independently are, of course, scattered throughout his career, but two obvious groupings of independent work are between the work with Beaumont and that with Massinger and toward the end of his life when Massinger himself began to write more independently. *Bonduca, The Honest Man's Fortune, Wit Without Money,* and *The Mad Lover* belong to the former group; *Rule a Wife and Have a Wife, A Wife for a Month, The Chances,* and *The Elder Brother* belong to the latter. *The Island Princess, The Pilgrim,* and *The Wild Goose Chase,* to name but three plays, were written independently during the period of collaboration with Massinger.

By any accounting John Fletcher, collaboratively and alone, was a productive playwright and an immensely successful one. His reputation matched and, hard as it is to believe, at times surpassed that of William Shakespeare. Although an adaptation of *The Custom of the Country* by Nicholas Wright was performed in London at the Barbican in 1983, that production is unlikely to herald a revival of stage interest in Fletcher.

Nonetheless, we can hardly ignore a dramatist who could claim both Ben Jonson's friendship and professional respect and at the same time collaborate with Shakespeare, and who, more significantly, was Shakespeare's successor. William Habington's praise of Fletcher as the "great tutelary Spirit of the Stage!" (Folio, b3v) we may write off as hyperbole, but Richard Brome, Ben Jonson's former servant and dramatic disciple, was a professional himself, one whose praise may be viewed as an accurate measure of the contemporary admiration paid Fletcher:

> His Scenes were Acts, and every Act a Play,
> I knew him in his strength; even then, when He
> That was the Master of his Art and Me
> Most knowing *Johnson* (proud to call him *Sonne*)
> In friendly Envy swore, He had out-done
> His very Selfe.
>
>   (Folio, g)

What Brome obviously admired was Fletcher's compacted dramatic intensity, his ability to fill the stage moment with excitement, his dramatic force. Sheer theatricality and an absolute sense and command of the stage are what still give life to many of his plays today. He was a consummate man of the theater. If his characters, themes, and scenes often seem quaint and dusty to readers three hundred years later, his skill transmutes the dust and familiarizes the quaintness. Fletcher's dramatic skill is still fresh and alive, and by transforming peculiar Stuart views of love and politics, honor and dishonor into living stage moments, he at the least holds a mirror to the past in which we may even, if we look closely, catch some glimpses of ourselves and our days. John Aubrey provides the sole account of Fletcher's death:

John Fletcher, invited to goe with a Knight into Norfolke or Suffolke in the Plague-time 1625, stayd but to make himselfe a suite of Cloathes, and while it was makeing, fell sick of the Plague and dyed. This I had (1668) from his Tayler, who is now a very old man, and Clarke of St. Mary Overy's in Southwark. Mr. Fletcher had an Issue in his arm (I thought it had not used so long ago). The Clarke (who was wont to bring him Ivy-leaves to dresse it) when he came, found the Spotts upon him. Death stopped his Journey and laid him low here.[24]

Chapter Two
Early Collaboration and Plays for the Children

Plays for the Boy Actors

John Fletcher began his dramatic career writing plays for the somewhat special audience of the private theaters and the boy actors. With the exception of *The Faithful Shepherdess* (1608–9) all the early plays considered in this chapter were collaborations with Francis Beaumont. Other plays for private theaters are *The Woman Hater* (1606), *The Coxcomb* (1607–10), *The Captain* (1609–12), *Cupid's Revenge* (1607–12), and *The Scornful Lady* (ca. 1610). But as always with Fletcher there are problems with dating and with assignments to acting companies. *Four Plays, or Moral Representations in One* (ca. 1608–13), a collaborative effort of Fletcher and probably Nathan Field, was not published separately and is not clearly identified as a play for boys although its music and dance have led to its being so considered. Four other plays—*Women Pleased, The Woman's Prize, or The Tamer Tamed, The Noble Gentleman,* and *Love's Cure*—have been dated as early as 1604 to 1606, but none of them was published before the folio of 1647, and later dates are finally more convincing. *The Little Thief* and *Monsieur Thomas* are also of uncertain date and might also have been written for the Children, but, since the question is open, they are treated elsewhere.

These necessary qualifications out of the way, we can look at the early plays themselves. The unifying feature of all the collaborative plays is in their theatricality. Individual scenes are usually more important than dramatic unity; the parts are greater than the whole. The actors' roles, in the sense of stage moments, are more important than the delineation of character; surfaces count more than depths. These characteristics, in general, remain throughout Fletcher's career. *The Faithful Shepherdess,* on the other hand, is far more poetic, "artistic," and highbrow; in short, deliberate coterie theater.

With the exception of *The Knight of the Burning Pestle* and *The*

Faithful Shepherdess, Beaumont and Fletcher showed early in their collaborative life an acute sense of the commercially theatrical. The initial plays establish the traits and subject matter that would make John Fletcher not merely a successful playwright, but the creator of a dominant theatrical tone and style. With the exception, moreover, of *Cupid's Revenge* and *The Faithful Shepherdess,* the plays are all comedies, and it is in comedy that Fletcher's greatest strengths are found.

Song, dance, and satire are frequent marks of plays written for the boy companies. Perhaps the most important characteristic of these plays is in the audience's awareness that the players are children. This awareness can be intensified or ignored as the dramatist (and indeed the player) wishes. Michael Shapiro notes that "The comedies acted by the children's troupes . . . are studded with various devices intended to remind the audiences of the actors behind the characters" and notes in particular "the use of adult actors alongside children," "bawdry," and "self-reference."[1] The reader of these plays needs to be constantly conscious of the possibilities of interpretation resulting from varying degrees of play with the audience's awareness that the actors are not just actors, but child actors.

The Woman Hater and *The Coxcomb*

An *olla podrida,* according to the *Oxford English Dictionary,* is "a dish of Spanish origin composed of pieces of many kinds of meat, vegetables, etc. stewed or boiled together." Such a description suits much of Fletcher's work. *The Woman Hater,* for instance, was written by Fletcher and Beaumont for the Children of Paul's in 1606 and published in 1607.[2] The main plot involves the attempts of the misogynist Gondarino to slander Oriana, beloved of the duke of Milan, and her victory over the slanderer. The subplot, which provides the comic star-turn of the play, recounts Lazarello's frantic attempts to dine on the head of the *umbrana,* a fish of rare delicacy. The ultimate cost of his gourmet dinner is marriage to a whore. A reissue of the quarto in 1649 subtitles the play "The Hungry Courtier," pointing to the popularity of his role.

Clearly the plot material of *The Woman Hater* is slight enough to raise the eyebrows of even a network television producer. Its pretensions, however, are not high. The prologue to the play sheds some light on the aims of the authors and is worth quoting at length:

If there be any amongst you, that come to heare lascivious Scenes, let them depart: for . . . you shall have no bawdrie in it: or if there be any lurking amongst you in corners, with Table bookes, who have some hope to find fit matter to feede his ———— malice on, let them claspe them up, and slinke away, or stay and be converted. . . . I dare not call it Comedie, or Tragedie; 'tis perfectly neyther: A Play it is, which was meant to make you laugh. . . . Some things in it you may meete with, which are out of the Common Roade: a Duke there is, and the Scene lyes in *Italy,* as those two thinges lightly wee never misse. But you shall not find in it the ordinarie and over-worne trade of jeasting at Lordes and Courtiers, and Citizens without taxation of any particular or new vice by them found out, but at the persons of them: such, he that made this, thinkes vile; and for his owne part vowes, That he did never thinke, but that a Lord born might be a wise man, and a Courtier an honest man. (*DW,* vol. 1; 157)

The claim that there is no bawdry stretches the point, but it asserts the author's rejection of the normal expectation of bawdry for the children. That the play is free from personal satire is another declaration of freedom from the expected conventions for plays written for boy actors. The comfortable acceptance of conventional setting and characterization, a duke and Italy, on the other hand, stresses an easy acceptance of unreality and a primary concern with entertainment of all sorts, a dramatic *olla podrida,* its limits only those claimed by a certain sense of propriety—no bawdry, no personal satire, and a proper respect for rank. On the other hand, one can argue that the prologue is one of those disclaimers designed to alert the audience to look for just such things as these.[3]

The Woman Hater is a comedy, not a tragicomedy, but its tone is mixed. Lazarello and Gondarino are both humors comedy characters, but while Lazarello is basically farcical, Gondarino's behavior and language range from the farcical to the pathological. The tone shifts accordingly from the high silliness of Lazarello's declaration of his desire "To see my loves face, the chast virgin head / Of a deere Fish, yet pure and undeflowered / Not known of man" (1.3.170) to Gondarino's cynical libertinism: "Count, thou art young, and inexperienced, in the darke hidden wayes of women: Thou dar'st affirme with confidence a Ladie of fifteene may be a maide" (5.4.230) to Arrigo's savage and bizarre threat during the test of Oriana's chastity: "I will injoy thee, though it be betweene the parting of thy soule and body" (5.4.230). The play moves among extremes

and freely mixes satire against government spies and references to
the Gunpowder Plot with romance, humors comedy, sexual dueling,
mild bawdry, melodrama, and farce. It is not a stew to all tastes
but it demonstrates the range of styles in the early collaborative
works and forecasts the mix of entertainment to come. The tonal
variations in the play are further enriched by the possibilities of self-
parody, always present in the audience's awareness, that the characters are portrayed by boys. Arrigo's lines, for example, have one
effect when growled in a bass voice by a fully grown man and quite
another when piped by a pink-cheeked prepubescent boy.

The one song in the play is by Fletcher and is a good example
of his early lyric strength:

> Come sleepe, and with thy sweet deceiving,
> Lock me in delight a while,
> Let some pleasing Dreames beguile
> All my fancies, that from thence
> I may feele an influence,
> All my powers of care bereaving.
>   (3.1.187)

Oriana sings this to Gondarino with an explanatory aside, "I had
rather sing at dores for bread, then sing to this fellow, but for hate:
if this should be told in the Court, that I begin to woe Lords, what
a troop of the untrust nobilitie should I have at my lodging to
morrow morning" (3.1.187). The aside, the song, and Gondarino's
churlish response, "Have you done your wassayle . . . I had as
leeve here a Catte cry, when her taile is cut off, as heare these
lamentations, these lowsie love-layes, these bewaylements" (3.1.188)
are variously qualified when we recall the boy actors.

The changes of tone are even more extreme in *The Coxcomb*.
Libertine comedy, pastoralism, romance, bawdry, and knock-about
farce are jumbled together in this rather unsure and uneven comedy
written between 1608 and 1610. An earlier private theater production may be assumed, but it was certainly acted at Court by the
Children of the Queen's Revels in November of 1612.[4] Beaumont
is credited with the romantic plot in which Viola agrees to elope
with Richardo, who arrives at their rendezvous drunk, accompanied
by equally drunken friends, and is arrested by the watch, leaving
Viola to the mercy of the night and a series of tribulations before

she is reunited with Richardo in a pastoral scene of repentance and forgiveness. Fletcher is responsible for the comic plot, based on Cervantes's tale of the willing cuckold, "The Curious Impertinent," from *Don Quixote.* Antonio (the coxcomb) is anxious to have his friend Mercury sleep with his wife so that he may demonstrate his exalted friendship: "If ever any had a faithfull friend I am that man, and I may glory in in't, this is he, that *ipse* he, that passes all Christendome for goodnesse, he shall not over go me in his friendship 'twere recreant and base . . . I am resolv'd, go thy wayes, a wife shall never part us, I have consider'd and finde her nothing to such a friend as thou art. . . . now to your taske, I give you free leave, and the sinne is mine if there be any in it" (*DW,* vol. 1; 2.1.289). Antonio is appropriately cuckolded but left unaware of it. His wife's reputation is preserved while Mercury (with a slight echo of *Hamlet*) is philosophically repentant:

> Udsfoote I am monstrous angry with my selfe:
> Why should a man that has discourse and reason,
> And knows how neere he looses all in these things,
> Covet to have his wishes satisfied;
> Which when they are, are nothing but the shame?
> (4.8.327)

The Coxcomb is a weak play; the carpentry joining the two plots is clumsy and neither plot carries great conviction. Nancy Cotton Pearse argues that the theme of the wife who commits adultery because her husband is such a great fool "is antipathetic to Fletcher's tendency to glorify chastity and results in . . . artistic failure" and objects to "the intrusion of inappropriate moralizing about a cuck-olding that the audience has previously been made to sympathize with."[5] Mercury's moralizing, however, is little more than a pro forma nod to virtue. (Surely there were some greybeards at the court performance ready to frown and cluck their way through plays like *The Coxcomb.*) Moreover, Mercury stops moralizing when Maria en-ters in her night dress—"Yet I shall forget my self againe; / I feele the Divell ready to hold my stirrop" (4.8.329)—and the scene ends on a note of mild sexual titillation. The real point of Mercury's moralizing is to demonstrate how tenuous it is when Maria shows up in her night clothes.

Finally, it is to scenes we must look in assessing the strengths of

The Coxcomb. None of the characters is especially memorable, but
there are a number of lively and varied stage moments. And again
the sheer variety of tone and style is impressive. Antonio's comic
anxiety to demonstrate his friendship by offering Mercury his wife
has already been mentioned. Viola, alone in the night with a little
casket of jewels stolen from her father and waiting for Richardo to
appear, is a figure of pathos set against a fine drinking scene in
which Richardo and his companions roar and call for whores:

> *Silvio.*   I, a good whore were worth money, boy.
>
> *Drawer.*   I protest Sir we are all together unprovided.
>
> *Richardo.* The mor's the pitty, boy; can you not vize us where, my
>   child?
>
> *Drawer.*   Neither, in troth Sir.
>
> *Pedro.*   Why where were you brought up boy? no inckling of a
>   whore? no ayme my boy?
>
> *Uberto.*   It cannot sink in my head now, that thou shouldst marry,
>   why shouldst thou marry, tell me?
>
> *Richardo.* I marry? Ile be hang'd first: some more wine boy (1.6.283)

Here is the "language of gentlemen" indeed. Drunk and lecherous
they swarm out of the tavern to find the innocent Viola:

> *Viola.*   Alas what are you? or what do you meane?
>   Sweet love wher's the place?
>
> *Richardo.* Mary sweet love, ee'n here; lye downe, Ile fease you.
>   (1.6.284)

But the timely entrance of the watch prevents a rape. It is a fine
mixture of realistic drunken comedy, pathos, melodrama, and, ar-
guably, satire. The scene is probably by Fletcher and shows his bent
for the dramatic and his command of realistic language. Admittedly
it is hard to stir up much enthusiasm for Antonio's comic Irishman
act, but the routine was fresher in the seventeenth century. The
following exchange, however, points to Fletcher's skilled sense of
comic timing and of dialogue tightly constructed for a punchline:

> *1 Servant.* Sir, will you be still an *Irish-man?*
>
> *Antonio.*   Yes a while.

> 2 *Servant.*   But your Worship will be beaten no more?
> *Antonio.*   No I thanke you *William.* (3.2.308)

The scenes of attempted rape might be read as moralistic attacks on drunkenness and lust and the contrast of the professions of gentlemen and their actual behavior, but titillation seems a more likely intent. A country gentleman, Valerio, rescues poor Viola from a pair of tinkers who tie her up and threaten to cut off her nose and eat it. Still, the relief of rescue is qualified by his lecherousness: "Alas! thou art young and tender, let me see thy hand, this was neere made to wash or wind up water, beate cloaths, or rub a floor, by this light, for one use that shall be namelesse, tis the best wanton hand that ere I lookt on" (2.2.296). We need not dwell on the reading a boy actor might give this line. The unabashed bawdiness is an inevitable part of the mix of voices in these plays.

Richardo repents his drunkenness, but *The Coxcomb* is hardly an attack on inebriety. Antonio is a fool, but his folly is artificial, unattached to any larger societal vision. The parody of exaggerated tales of friendship is incidental. Neither *The Woman Hater* nor *The Coxcomb* pretends to anything more than entertainment. Both make appropriate use of the possibilities of the boy actors. Both look forward to repeated tones and patterns of later work.

The Faithful Shepherdess

It is in *The Faithful Shepherdess* that Fletcher pretends to far more than entertainment. The play was published in an undated quarto around 1609. Fletcher's address "To the Reader" reflects his irritation at the unfavorable reception of the play in performance. His annoyance at being misunderstood led him to describe his intentions and the kind of play he had written.

If you be not reasonably assurde of your knowledge in this kind of Poeme, lay down the book or read this, which I wish had bene the prologue. It is a pastorall Tragie-comedie, which the people seeing when it was plaid . . . concluded to be a play of country hired Shepheards, in gray cloakes, with curtaild dogs in strings, sometimes laughing together, and sometimes killing one another: And missing whitsun ales, creame, wassel and morris-dances, began to be angry. . . . Understand . . . a pastorall to be a representation of shepheards and shepheardesses, with their actions and passions, which must be such as may agree with their natures, at least not exceeding former fictions, and vulgar traditions: they are not to be adorn'd with any art, but such improper ones as nature is said to bestow, as singing and Poetry, or such as experience may teach them, as the vertues of hearbs, and fountaines, the ordinary course of the Sun, moone, and starres, and such like. But you are ever to remember Shepherds to be such, as all the ancient Poets and moderne of understanding have receaved them: that is, the owners of flockes and not hyerlings. A tragie-comedie is not so called in respect of mirth and killing, but in respect it wants deaths, which is inough to make it no tragedie, yet brings some neere it, which is inough to make it no comedie: which must be a representation of familiar people, with such kinde of trouble as no life be questiond, so that a God is as lawfull in this as in a tragedie, and meane people as in a comedie. Thus much I hope will serve to justifie my Poeme, and make you understand it. To teach you more for nothing, I do not know that I am in conscience bound. (*DW*, vol. 3;497)

Fletcher's pastoral, then, was to be seen as an aristocratic entertainment with aristocratic, or at least gentrified, protagonists, "owners of flockes and not hyerlings." It was also so new a form, so far from the audience's expectations that it required definition. Neither the pastoral nor tragicomedy were really new. The newness lay in the treatment and in the author's consciousness of working in a particular genre with a critical doctrine attached to it as opposed to a gallimaufrey of tragic and comic action with rustic shepherds on the side.

A number of influences are evident in *The Faithful Shepherdess* including Edmund Spenser's *The Faerie Queene, The Arcadia* of Sir Philip Sidney, and Shakespeare's *A Midsummer Night's Dream*, but the title and the critical doctrine derive from *Il Pastor Fido* (The faithful shepherd), a pastoral tragicomedy written in 1585 by Giovanni Battista Guarini. By 1602—the time of the English translation—twenty Italian editions of this highly admired work had been published. Guarini quickly achieved such fashionable popularity in England that Ben Jonson has Lady Would-be in *Volpone* remark that English writers steal almost as much from Guarini as from Montaigne: "He has so moderne, and facile a veine, / Fitting the time, and catching the court-eare."[6]

Guarini responded to attacks on his play and theories in 1601 with *Il compendio della poesia tragicomica* (The compendium of tragicomic poetry) in which he argued for tragicomedy as a new and superior genre able to replace the outworn genres of comedy and tragedy: "And just as the age changes, habits change. . . . And to come to our age, what need have we today to purge terror and pity with tragic sights, since we have the precepts of our most holy religion, which teaches us with the word of the gospel? Hence these horrible and savage spectacles are superfluous, nor does it seem to me that we should introduce tragic action for any other reason than to get delight from it."[7] Guarini's definition of tragicomedy undoubtedly influenced Fletcher: "He who composes tragicomedy takes from tragedy its great persons but not its great action, its verisimilar plot but not its true one, its movement of the feelings but not its disturbance of them, its pleasure but not its sadness, its danger but not its death; from comedy it takes laughter that is not excessive, modest amusement, feigned difficulty, happy reversal, and above all the comic order."[8]

In *The Faithful Shepherdess* Fletcher, then, was consciously writing in a new and fashionable theatrical style and form. Eventually tragicomedy, featuring turnings of plot, concentration on the movement of varieties of emotions, and self-conscious theatricality, would set the tone of Jacobean drama. Thus the answer to why *The Faithful Shepherdess*, a play aimed so carefully at a literate, modern, courtly, and sophisticated audience, at first failed is not certain. Perhaps the best answer is that the Blackfriars audience was just not courtly or sophisticated enough. In the poem that he wrote for the quarto edition of the play Ben Jonson describes the audience in biting terms:

> The wise, and many-headed *Bench,* that sits
>   Upon the Life, and Death of *Playes,* and *Wits,*
> (Compos'd of *Gamester, Captaine, Knight, Knight's man,*
>   *Lady,* or *Pusil,* that weares maske, or fan,
> *Velvet,* or *Taffata* cap, rank'd in the darke
>   With the shops *Foreman,* or some such *brave sparke,*
> That may judge for his *six-pence*) had before
>   They saw it halfe, damnd thy whole play. . . .
>   (*DW,* Vol. 3;492)

The composition of the audience, the darkened auditorium, and the price all indicate Blackfriars and a so-called coterie audience rather than the Globe. According to Jonson, at least in this case the coterie was not very select. As Andrew Gurr points out, however, "shortly afterwards the King's Men took over the theatre [Blackfriars] and

performed Beaumont and Fletcher's *Philaster,* a modified version of
the same kind of play, which had an enormous success and created
a fashion for tragi-comedy to out-last the Stuart reign."⁹

The real problem for *The Faithful Shepherdess,* then, may have been
in its pastoral rather than its tragicomic mode and in the play's
poetic rather than dramatic language. It may simply have been too
courtly, even for the audience of a children's company at a private
theater. It was successfully revived and played at court in the reign
of Charles I and has since maintained a modest appeal. Sir Thomas
Beecham produced a lavish revival in 1923, and two decades later
Glynne Wickham directed a successful abridged version on radio
for the British Broadcasting Corporation.

The Faithful Shepherdess mixes the pastoral world of shepherd and
shepherdess, satyrs, and Pan with a fairyland of enchantments, magic
wells, transformations, and miraculous cures. The play's center is
provided by the shepherdess Clorin who has vowed to devote her
life to mourning her dead lover through her chaste and pious acts.
She is aided in her endeavors by a Puck-like satyr overcome by her
beauty and virtue. The gentle behavior of "this rude man, and beast"
leads Clorin to reflect on a major theme of the play:

> sure there is a power
> In that great name of virgin, that bindes fast
> All rude uncivill bloods, all appetites
> That breake their confines: then, strong chastity,
> Be thou my strongest guarde, for heere Il'e dwell
> In opposition against Fate and Hell.
>
> (1.1.504)

The action begins in the afternoon following a festival in honor
of Pan and extends through the night. Various sets of shepherds
and shepherdesses arrange to meet in the woods. The chaste Amoret,
for example, agrees to join her lover Perigot in the grove by

> A vertuous Well, about whose flowery bancks,
> The nimble footed Faeries dance their rounds,
> By the pale moone-shine, dipping often times
> Their stolen children, so to make them free
> From dying flesh and, dull mortalitie. . . .
>
> (1.2.507)

where shepherds and shepherdesses also come to plight their troths. A complication is introduced when Amarillis declares to Perigot her love for him and is swiftly rejected. Amarillis is not a girl who accepts refusal: "I must not leave to love, / I cannot, no, I must enjoy thee, boy" (1.2.510), and when the Sullen Shepherd, "One that doth weare himselfe away in lonenesse, / And never joyes unlesse it be in breaking / The holy plighted troth of mutuall soules" (1.2.510), asks for her love, she agrees to grant it if he will help her to separate Perigot from Amoret.

Two other types of lovers are represented by Cloe and Thenot. Cloe is desperately searching for a lover, any lover at all, while Thenot is in love with Clorin, "the virgin of the grove," because of her loyalty to her dead lover. Cloe is not the least interested in chastity nor its admirers and expresses her views in a song, "Come, Shepheards, come," which ends

> Now, or never
> Come and have it,
> Thinke not I
> Dare deny,
> If you crave it.
> (1.3.514)

She arranges to meet Daphnis in the grove, but is deeply disappointed when he assures her of his purity. She is delighted when Alexis, who holds absolutely no brief for chastity, arrives and also agrees to meet her in the grove.

When the Priest of Pan gives the evening benediction and instructs the shepherds and shepherdesses to fold their flocks and go to bed, they have in fact all arranged meetings in the woods. Now the night, reminiscent of *A Midsummer Night's Dream,* is filled with confusions, dangers, and contretemps of love, holy and unholy. The Sullen Shepherd, the embodiment of naturalistic lust, arrives to meet Amarillis and declares his undifferentiated desire for all women:

> all to me in sight
> Are equall; be they faire, or blacke, or browne,
> Virgin, or carelesse wanton, I can crowne
> My appetite with any: sweare as oft,
> And weepe as any, melt my words as soft
> Into a maidens eares, and tell how long

> My heart has bene her servant, and how strong
> My passions are: call her unkinde and cruell,
> Offer her all I have to gaine the jewell
> Maidens so highly praise: then loath and fly:
> This do I hold a blessed desteny.
>
> (2.3.525)

There is something of the early John Donne here and something
purely melodramatic; both aspects are immeasurably enriched and
complicated by the reedy voice of the boy actor or contrariwise by
the masculine voice of an adult playing the role in the company of
children. The plan to win Perigot that Amarillis explains to the
Sullen Shepherd involves changing her appearance into that of Amoret, a transformation that can be effected by the proper charm and
by being dipped into the magic well.

The pastoral world of Guarini has now in large measure been
replaced by the magical fairyland of Spenser and the moonlight
confusions of Shakespeare. Amarillis's transformation is an effective
piece of stage business, making use of the trapdoor and a switch in
actors. The false Amoret, like the false Una in *The Faerie Queene*,
now sets out to seduce Perigot, and the Sullen Shepherd sends the
true Amoret on a false trail after Perigot. The Sullen Shepherd
immediately regrets sending her away:

> Why did not I assay to win her love?
> She would not sure have yeilded unto me,
> Woemen love onely opportunitie
> And not the man, or if she had denied,
> Alone, I might have forced her to have tried
> Who had bene stronger: O vaine foole, to let
> Such lest occasion passe: Ile follow yet,
> My blood is up, I cannot now forbeare.
>
> (3.1.535)

The Sullen Shepherd's libertine nastiness is compounded when
he comes upon Cloe and Alexis who have just begun cuddling. He
stabs Alexis and demands Cloe but runs off when the Satyr makes
a timely entrance. This Satyr has nothing to do with the Renaissance
associations of satyrs with satire but derives in the main from Puck
and plays the role of a sylvan Boy Scout:

> heere must I stay,
> To see what mortalls loose their way,
> And by a false fire, seeming bright,
> Traine them in and leave them right:
> Then must I watch if any be
> Forcing of a chastity,
> If I finde it, then in haste,
> Give my wreathed horn a blast
> And the faieries all will run,
> Wildely dauncing to the moone,
> And wil pinch him to the bone,
> Till his lustfull thoughts be gone.
>
> (3.1.537)

The Satyr then takes Alexis off to Clorin to be cured.

Meanwhile, Cloe has not been frightened nor her desires cooled by her immediate adventures: "It is Impossible to Ravish mee, I am soe willing . . ." (3.1.538), she asserts in one of those surefire lines that so disgusted Charles Lamb.[10] But in this Fletcher merely follows Guarini, who makes his own naughty shepherdess, Corisca, essentially comic. Squirrellike, Cloe has stowed away her extra, although disappointingly chaste, lover, Daphnis, in a hollow tree, and she decides to try to cure him of his chastity and fashion him into a suitable replacement for Alexis.

Perigot and Amarillis (as "Amoret") now have one of the major scenes in the play. Unlike Lysander in *A Midsummer Night's Dream*, Perigot does not even think of lying down with his love on a grassy bank but stipulates they lie apart. The passage in which he does so illustrates Fletcher's stylistic variety, here the poetic evocation of an enchanted and innocent fairyland:

> here shalt thou rest
> Uppon this holy bancke: no deadly snake,
> Uppon this Turffe her selfe in foulds doth make,
> Here is no poyson, for the Toade to feed.
> Here boldly spread thy handes, no venomd weed
> Dares blister them. No slymy snaile dare creepe,
> Over thy face when thou art fast a sleepe,
> Here never durst the bablinge Cuckoe spitt.
> No slough of falling starr did ever hitt
> Upon this Bancke. Let this thy Cabin bee;
> This other set with violets for mee.
>
> (3.2.539)

This is not, however, the sort of nocturn the False Amoret had in mind, and she horrifies Perigot with her raw masculine libertinism:

> Still thinkst thou such a thinge as Chastitie
> Is amongst woemen? *Perigot,* thers none,
> That with her love is in a wood alone,
> And wood come home a Mayde; be not abusd,
> With thy fond first beleife. . . .
>
> (3.2.540)

The clash of language and the reversal of roles make a lively scene brilliantly culminated in a series of reversals. Perigot, deeply shocked, resolves to kill the false Amoret, draws his sword, and chases her off the stage: "This steele shall peirse thy lustfull hart" (3.2.541).

The Sullen Shepherd now handily returns Amarillis to her own shape. When the real Amoret enters, Perigot, crying "Death is the best reward thats due to lust" (3.2.542), stabs her. The Sullen Shepherd, fearing that some officious busybody might chance by and save her, dumps her in the well. His murderous intent, however, is foiled, for *"The* God of the River *Riseth with* Amoret, *in his armes"* (3.2.543). Because she is "an unpoluted maid," he is able to cure her immediately and is so taken with her that he proposes that she join him in a watery marriage in the river. Amoret politely declines his invitation, saying she must continue to follow Perigot.

The River God's language provides still another poetic shift:

> Not a fish in all my brooke,
> That shall disobeye thy looke,
> But when thou will come slyding bye,
> And from thy white hand take a flye. . . .
>
> (3.2.544)

His attractive song closely parallels William Browne's narrative poem *Brittania's Pastoral* (1613).[11]

One final twist is given to the action before the night ends. In his grief Perigot is ready to commit suicide when Amarillis stops him by explaining that Amoret has always been chaste and true and that she herself had slandered her by appearing in her very form and likeness. Amarillis promises to demonstrate her powers of transformation. Before she can do so, however, Amoret, now cured of her wounds by the River God, encounters Perigot, who, assuming that the real Amoret is Amarillis transformed, becomes enraged at her protestations of love, devotion, and chastity and stabs her once more, anticipating the double stabbing in *Philaster*.

The useful Satyr takes Amoret to Clorin for help and all is eventually resolved. Thenot, the shepherd who loves Clorin because she is faithful to her dead lover and can never love him, is cured when Clorin pretends to love Thenot. He is furiously disillusioned—"thou art of women's race and full of guilt" (4.5.564)—and abandons love and love melancholy. Clorin clarifies her motives when she declares, "I rather chuse, though I a woman bee, / He should speake ill of all, than dye for me" (4.5.564). The tone of all this is sometimes difficult to gauge. It can seem serious, but the real point is obviously in the paradox—the lover who will love only as long as the beloved does not love.

Meanwhile, Clorin has cured Alexis of *his* wounds, but warns him that lustful thoughts can reopen them. (Clearly there is play throughout *The Faithful Shepherdess* with the conceit that the literary metaphor of "love's wounds" has been literalized; the spirit is made flesh.) The Satyr now brings in Amoret and Clorin undertakes her cure, "With spotlesse hand on spotlesse Brest, / I put these hearbs to give thee rest" (5.2.567). But the herbs do not work and Amoret's chastity is suspected: "thou art not sound, / Full of lust" (5.2.567). It is one more turn of the theatrical knife for Amoret, but the impurity is quickly attributed to Cloe and Daphnis when they are discovered in a hollow tree. They are given a test for purity—if the flame of a candle (easily seen in the dark enclosure of the private theater) moves away from one's hand and does not burn it, chastity is established. Daphnis easily passes, but Cloe fails. To cap it all, Alexis's wounds reopen.

Amarillis rushes onto the stage with the Sullen Shepherd in lustful pursuit. She has undergone an unexplained but complete conversion:

> I am not now,
> That wanton *Amarillis:* heere I vowe,
> To Heaven, and thee, grave father, if I may
> Scape this unhappy Night, to know the day
> A virgin, never after to endure
> The tongues, or company of men unpure.
>
> (5.3.572)

The Priest of Pan takes the thoroughly unrepentant Sullen Shepherd into custody.

The stage direction for the last scene establishes a final tableau: *"The Curtayne is drawne,* Clorin *appeares sitting in the Cabin,* Amoret *sitting on the one side of her,* Alexis *and* Cloe *on the other, the* Satyre *standing by"* (5.5.575). The scene awaits only Perigot and Amarillis to complete the icon. Alexis and Cloe (who has now been cured of lust) declare their chaste love and then Perigot arrives with bloody hands and regrets for the recognition scene with Amoret and for his ritual cleansing. This accomplished, Amarillis is brought in and passes the test for purity. The night, with its lusts, confusions, trials, and dangers, is over. The shepherds and shepherdesses are united, the Sullen Shepherd is banished, and the order of chaste love is restored.

What should appear from this summary above all is the variety of stage action in *The Faithful Shepherdess,* its pleasure in tricks and turns. Perhaps less evident is the variety of language, but the voices in the play are many. The Sullen Shepherd is basically the spokesman for libertine naturalism, but can eloquently speak the language of the Petrarchan lover for purposes of seduction. The Satyr in varied meters calls up Puck and fairyland. Perigot and Amoret command a multitude of rhetorics from the pathetic to the melodramatic.

For Fletcher's audience, at least for the literarily sophisticated, the tone of the play would also be effected by its interconnections with the variety of texts it draws upon and interacts with. This is not the place for an exhaustive study of the intertextualities involved, but links with works by Sidney, Spenser, Shakespeare, and Guarini have been touched upon, and the acting and reading of the play would have been influenced by its relation to these texts. The libertine verse of the early John Donne provides yet another text to consider. Fletcher himself points to the newness of Guarini's theories, to a conscious modernity. Yet pastoralism is nostalgic, looking back to an idyllic, preurbanized past. Guarini asserts the Christian basis of tragicomedy. How do all these aspects work for Fletcher and for his audience?

Surely the very land itself would influence the creation and response to the play. Anyone visiting Penshurst, the Kentish great house of the Sidney family, cannot but be struck with the appropriateness of Sidney's *Arcadia* to it. Even today sheep graze in its park; one has only to glance out a window or to step out the door to be reminded of the pastoral, a pastoral preeminently aristocratic. Open fields and the vision of Arcadia were a stroll away from Fletcher's London, and the country intruded as herdsmen drove their livestock into the city markets. In short, playing at shepherd and shepherdess and evoking the Arcadian world was still a natural enough aristocratic pastime. The play needs to be read against that consciousness. Finally we should remind ourselves once more that the play was written for and acted by children.

W.W. Greg once commented astutely that "It is impossible to read *The Faithful Shepherdess* without being struck by the almost entire want of dramatic effect, for the situation at the end is for all purposes exactly what it was at the beginning. On the other hand, any one who takes the trouble to analyze the play scene by scene cannot help being struck by the astounding ingenuity with which the web of intrigue is woven and opportunity afforded for striking scenes and situations."[12] The latter is precisely the great merit of the play. The situation, moreover, has changed to the extent that the Sullen Shepherd is banished, the Arcadian innocence is grievously threatened by unchecked self-gratification, and libertine lawlessness has been preserved. Arcadia remains Arcadia, but does so because of the trials of the night. The essence of tragicomedy is that it asserts the lack of change, "the danger, not the death," the comic restoration and preservation of an essentially positive status quo.

Most likely the Blackfriars audience was unprepared for aristocratic pastoralism and the unrealistic ideality of the play. The Arcadia of *The Faithful Shepherdess* is too little grounded in the real world. The Forest of Arden has bad weather and is never far from that real world to which one must always return. The night's wonders of *A Midsummer Night's Dream* are perhaps all the more real because they are questioned in the broad prosaic light of the morning. Dramatically, the spirit of the masque too controls *The Faithful Shepherdess*. Its pleasures are decorative and better suited even to an evening at Whitehall than one at Blackfriars. "This Iron age that eates it selfe, will never / Bite at your golden world" (*DW*, Vol. 3;493), wrote George Chapman, Fletcher's fellow poet and playwright, in his dedicatory poem.

Fletcher's disappointment at the play's failure, then, must have been partially mollified by its publication, praise from Ben Jonson, and Chapman's recognition that *The Faithful Shepherdess* was "both a Poeme and a play." If it was a theatrical failure, it could be

assumed a poetic success. *The Faithful Shepherdess* is significant in
the development of Fletcher's theater, especially as an initial tragicomic statement. Beyond that it also remains a play of considerable
interest and momentary charm.

Cupid's Revenge

Like *The Faithful Shepherdess, Cupid's Revenge* draws on Sidney's
Arcadia for portions of its plot and its concern, in part at least, with
love. It too was acted by the Children of Her Majesty's Revels. It
was performed at court in 1612 and in 1613 and first published in
1615. *Cupid's Revenge* was written between 1607 and 1612 with a
strong case for the earlier date based on allusions to the expropriation
of the property of recusants (Roman Catholics who refused to take
sacraments in the Church of England) and to the execution of conspirators in the Gunpowder Plot.[13] Unlike *The Faithful Shepherdess,*
it is a tragedy as well as a collaborative effort, about equally divided
between Beaumont and Fletcher.

But *Cupid's Revenge* is a tragedy for its deaths rather than for any
sustained tragic feeling it evokes. Melodrama, comic satire, and a
touch of romance are the dominant notes. It is a rather patchy work
that switches style and tone from a masquelike opening with the
theme of the violation of or insult to the power of love to a revenge
play of sexual and political corruption with the motif of the cast-
off mistress of the son becoming the wife of his father, the Duke,
and the consequent destruction of all of them.

The play opens in the pagan world of romance with the promise
of Leontius, the doting Duke of Licia, to grant his daughter Hidaspes
any wish on her birthday. This straightlaced virgin requests that
Cupid's altars, "these erected obsceane Images" "May be pluckt
downe and burnt: and every man / That offers to 'em any sacrifice, /
May lose his life" (*DW,* vol. 2: 1.1.357). Leontius, whose judgment
is every bit as poor as King Lear's and whom in someways he recalls,
not only grants the request, but vows to grant Hidaspes another
wish.

The Duke's decision naturally upsets the courtiers and gives rise
to their witty and bawdy complaints. The Priest of Cupid, his boy,
and two attending couples enter to dance and sing *"Lovers rejoyce,
your pains shall be rewarded"* (1.2.341). The interruption of these
rites by the Duke's agents brings the sound of cornets and the
spectacular descent of Cupid and his curse:

> *Cupid's* revenge is mightie; with this arrow,
> Hotter than plagues or mine owne anger, will I
> Now nobly right my selfe: nor shall the prayers
> Nor sweete smokes on my Altars hold my hand,
> Till I have left this a most wretched land.
>
> (1.3.343)

And leave it so the god does. Immediately Hidaspes falls in love with her brother's dwarf, Zoylus, one who, as Hidaspes's maid declares, "will hardly / Serve i'th' darke when one is drunke" (1.4.345). (In the equivalent scene in Sidney's *Arcadia* the princess falls in love with a commoner.) The dwarf adds a bizarre sexual twist and a theatricality suitable to the boy actors. The Duke is naturally appalled when his daughter claims marriage with Zoylus as the second promise due her. Duke Leontius promptly orders Zoylus executed. The grief-stricken Hidaspes has only a brief death-bed scene in the second act; and the action and Cupid's revenge, as Cupid himself declares when he makes another descent at the beginning of act 2, turn to her brother Leucippus.

Cupid makes a perfunctory, masquelike descent—again with cornets—in act 5, but the idea that the action is controlled by the revenge of the god is largely forgotten. The play becomes a dynastic tragedy with a plotting, vicious, power-hungry, and sexually corrupt stepmother, a foolish and infatuated old father, and a maligned son with a prince-in-exile and a loyal and loving girl disguised as a page added for good measure.

Prince Leucippus has spent the night with Bacha, a new, beautiful but corrupt, widow. Bacha weeps crocodile tears over the loss of her honor, a commodity it is unlikely she ever had, but in soliloquy reveals her mercenary and Machiavellian motives, "being poore, / Ile both enjoy his bodye and his purse, / And he a Prince, nere thinke myselfe the worse" (2.2.354). The crucial complication comes when Duke Leontius confronts the guilty couple and Leucippus, in one of those complex paradoxes that so enchanted the age, lies outrageously in defense of Bacha's honor with the horrific result that his silly father falls in love with Bacha and sends Leucippus off to the wars, out of harm's and Bacha's way. The chivalrous lie leads straight to the tragic denouement.

Leontius is transformed into an absurd pantaloon: "O but since, his Taylor came, and they have fallen out about the fashion on's

cloathes: and yonders a fellow come, has board a hole in's eare; and
he has bespake a Vauting-horse, you shall see him come foorth
presently: he lookes like Winter, stucke here and there with fresh
flowers" (2.4.360). To the news that his daughter is dying, the
love-crazed old man replies: "Let her be so, I have other matters in
hand: but this same Taylor angers me, he has made my dublet so
wide: and see, the knave has put no points on my arm" (2.4.361).
This scene (it is Fletcher's) is grotesquely comic. What pathos might
be found in Hidaspes's death scene that immediately follows is
certainly qualified by the unambiguous tone of her maid's prayer
to Cupid:

> *Cupid* pardon what is past,
> And forgive our sinnes at last,
> Then we will be coye no more,
> But thy Deitie Adore,
> Troths at fifteene wee will plight,
> And will tread a Dance each night,
> In the Fields, or by the Fire,
> With the youths that have desire.
>   (2.5.363)

Somehow this just does not seem to strike a deeply tragic note.
    The Duke's marriage to Bacha markedly, if temporarily, improves
his health. He tells his flatterer Telamon that he has grown "Lustier,
I thanke thee for't, since I'm marryed; / I can stand now alone . . . /
And never stagger" (3.2.370). But Bacha will shortly give the silly
old Duke plenty to stagger about. She attempts to seduce Leucippus,
arguing ingeniously that "though I should lye with you, it is no
Lust, / For it desires no change, I could with you content my selfe"
(3.2.373). Leucippus's indignation is increased when Bacha offers
to kill the Duke if Leucippus will agree to marry her. The rejected
and furious Bacha now begins her plot to destroy Leucippus and
make her daughter, Urania, the heir to the dukedom. She convinces
Duke Leontius that Leucippus is plotting against him, and the Duke
has him arrested and condemns him to death. The citizens, loyal
to Leucippus, rescue him from jail.
    The scenes with the citizens, true-born Englishmen all, are at-
tributed to Fletcher and call to mind Thomas Dekker as well as the
popular theater that Beaumont parodied in *The Knight of the Burning
Pestle:* "Shut up my shop, and bee ready at a call boyes, and one of

you runne over my olde tucke with a few ashes, tis growne odious with tosting cheese: and burne a little giniper in my murrin. The maide made it her chamber-pot: an houre hence Ile come againe; and as you here from me, send me a cleane shirt" (4.3.397).

The language is inescapably parodic. The shift in tone and deliberate self-consciousness helps to qualify and sophisticate the reading of the tragedy. Leucippus refuses to revenge himself on Bacha and goes into exile, to the grief of his loyal friend, Ismenus: "Poxe o'me selfe for an Asse, Ime crying now, God be with you, if I never see you againe: why then pray get you gone, for grief and anger wonnot let me know what I say" (4.5.402). If this is not an overtly parodic moment, certainly the potential is there. When the Duke dies, Ismenus is ready with a wonderful burst of invective aimed at Bacha: "You fleering harlot, Ile have a horse to leape thee, and thy base issue shall carry Sumpters. Come Lords, bring her along, weele to the Prince all, where her hell-hood shall waite his censure; and if he spare thee she Goat, may he lye with thee againe; and beside, mayst thou lay upon him some nastie foule disease that hate still followes, and his end, a dry ditch. Leade you corrupted whore, or Ile draw gode shall make you skippe: away to the Prince" (5.2.406). Here is sheer delight in words and in inventive vituperation.

Leucippus is joined in exile by Bacha's daughter, Urania, a simple, good-hearted girl, raised in the country, who speaks a plain rustic dialect and shares none of the wicked traits of her mother. Urania has, of course, disguised herself as a page. The scene which Urania and Leucippus play aims perhaps at a sort of innocent pathos, but not without a degree of innuendo. "Ile come to thee Boy. / (This is a love I never yet heard tell of) . . ." (5.4.408). After Urania sings a song, the time-serving Timantus attempts to stab Leucippus. Urania steps between them and is wounded. Chastened, Timantus reveals himself and his murderous intentions. Leucippus challenges him to a duel, but Timantus treacherously wounds Leucippus when he is not looking. Leucippus in turn stabs Timantus and the following colloquy takes place:

> *Leucippus.* What course would you have taken when thou hadst killed me?
>
> *Timantus.* I would have tane your Page, and married her.
>
> *Leucippus.* What Page?
>
> *Timantus.* Your boy there. — [*Dyes.*] (5.4.411)

Recognition is not far behind, but Urania expires and echoes of
Hamlet begin to drum on the ears. Leucippus's instructions to Is-
menus for the disposition of Bacha are to "Leave her to heaven brave
Cousen" (5.4.412). Bacha now stabs Leucippus and then herself.
Quotation of the closing lines of the play is irresistible for the jarring
counterpoint of tones:

Leucippus.	Next to you Couzen *Ismenus,*
	That shall be the Duke, I pray you let
	The broken image of *Cupid* be reedified,
	I know all this is done by him.
Ismenus.	It shall be so.
Leucippus.	Last, I beseech you that my Mother-in-Law
	May have buriall according to— [*Dyes.*]
Ismenus.	To what sir?
Dorialus.	There is a full point.
Ismenus.	I will interpret for him; she shal have buriall
	According to her owne deserts, with dogs.
Dorialus.	I would your Majestie would haste for setling of the
	people.
Ismenus.	I am ready.
	Agenor, goe and let the Trumpets sound
	Some mournefull thing, whilst we convey the body
	Of this unhappy Prince unto the Court,
	And of that vertuous Virgin to a grave:
	But dragge her to a ditch, where let her lye
	Accurst, whilst one man has a memory.

                                                        (5.4.414)

No amount of trumpets will lend *Cupid's Revenge* tragic dignity
and power. Echoes of *Hamlet* will not change Leucippus from a
conventional cardboard figure into a tragic hero. To say that the
ending of *Cupid's Revenge* is rhetorical, that its effect rests entirely
on the language, is to make the point that will necessarily be
repeated over and over about Fletcher's plays. Effects are primary;
rhetoric matters more than meaning. *Cupid's Revenge* is a tragedy
because the action generates corpses. It could as easily have been
a tragicomedy by removing the killings and reforming the villainess.

The play has been read on the one hand as ridiculing chastity and on the other as a play showing the disastrous consequences of lust.[14] But theme is much less important than manner. The play, admittedly a weak one, is filled with matter and method appropriate to the private theaters and to the boy actors. The Cupid material is essentially abandoned after the first act, but the masquelike effects—the descent from the heavens, the cornets—associate the play with aristocratic and courtly entertainment. Bacha is a thoroughly stagey villainess loaded with vices. Lust is not enough for her. First she seduces the son, then the father, and then she attempts to win the son again. The audience is not allowed to forget the incest. Her lust extends to power and she will do anything to achieve it. The possibilities in the role are extensive and they are increased because a boy is playing it against other boy actors.

The satirical parts in the play are carried in particular by the time-serving courtier Timanthus and by a number of curious topical references. When the dwarf Zoylus is executed, for example, the courtiers dwell in some detail on the manner of his execution. In the article cited earlier, James Savage takes this to be a reference to the cruelty of the executions of the conspirators of the Gunpowder Plot. Beaumont had family connections with some of the conspirators; the house frequented by the conspirators was owned by his first cousin, Anne Vaux. "Would I had gin an hundred pound for a tolleration, that I might use my conscience in mine owne house" (1.1.338), Nisus declares as Leontius agrees to the destruction of Cupid's altars, a reference, Savage indicates, to a fee recusants might pay to avoid expropriation of their lands. The reference becomes even more pertinent when it is recalled that Beaumont's brother John had two thirds of his estate of Grace Dieu expropriated and granted to a courtier. In this light the whole plot of Hidaspes's destruction of the religion of Cupid and subsequent ruin of the kingdom may well take on a dangerous allegory. One act of such dark allusions would be more than enough and sufficient reason to abandon that plot line. "Priest change your coat you had best . . . learne to lye, and thrive" (1.2.341), Nilo tells the Priest of Cupid. Such lines would ring harshly in the ears of secret Catholics in the audience.

Cupid's Revenge is a play of considerable interest but certainly not one of Fletcher's stronger works. Still, it provides a point of reference for later tragedies and reminds us of the complexity of the texts of Fletcher's plays.

The Captain and The Scornful Lady

The Captain was written between 1609 and 1612 and was performed by the King's Men at court in 1612–31. It was first published in the 1647 folio.[15] There is no evidence of a production for a children's troop; but Lelia, "a cunning wanton widow," and her old father, not unlike Bacha and her old husband, are suitable roles for children, and the bawdry (or the "disgusting prurience")[16] of the scenes in which Lelia attempts to seduce her father is certainly suggestive of plays written for the boy actors as are the songs. At any rate The Captain belongs to the private and not the public stage and demonstrates such a mix of dramatic style that the Prologue declares, "This is nor Comody, nor Tragedy, / Nor History" (DW, vol. 1;551).

Some critics will add it is not even good red herring. It is difficult to call it even a tragicomedy in spite of tragicomic moments. It is another olla podrida, with mostly comic ingredients in the mix and theatricality once more the key ingredient. It is an uneven work with a few strong scenes and two good acting roles in Lelia and Jacomo, the captain of the title. Both roles are broad types, closer to caricature than character, but both have lengthy scenes in which interpretative opportunities, one for high villainy and the other for farcical comedy, are substantial.

The comic Jacomo is identified in the list of characters as "an angry Captain, a Woman-hater." The identification is misleading and has misled some commentators. He is not in fact a woman hater, but acts the part because he expects to be ridiculed for his face which is "no better than a ragged Map . . . / Of where I have marcht and traveled" and particularly for his legs thin as "a paire of cat-sticks" (2.1.572). Jacomo is a bluff and seasoned soldier, but self-conscious and shy with women in a time of peace.

He is beloved by a young woman named Franck. The comic plot leads to their marriage, its consummation arrived at by strange and devious paths. Two "Cowardly Gulls," fops in another age, Lodowicke and Piso, plot for reasons not very well developed to get Jacomo drunk. He naturally outdrinks them both in a vigorous and realistic tavern scene filled with enough "Anons!" to recall Shakespeare's Henry IV, part 1. After he has outdrunk the two gulls, Franck and her allies trap him so that she can declare her love and win this shy soldier. When he is drunk, he has the courage to approach the ladies, kissing even Franck's friend Clora, and complimenting her with high courtship:

> *Jacomo.* One tast more o' your office: go thy wayes
> With thy small kettle Drumes; upon my conscience
> Thou art the best, that e're a man laid his leg o'er.
>
> *Clora.* He smells just like a Cellar, fye upon him.
>
> (4.3.618)

As well as kissing Clora and Franck, he kisses Fredrick, Franck's brother, but he is infuriated when Fredrick laughs at him and lunges at him with his sword. Fredrick feigns death. Jacomo is taken off to sober up. Once sober Jacomo is too ashamed to face Franck, who has not been dissuaded from her love by his behavior.

> *Clora.* Now *Franck,* see what kind of man you love,
> That loves you when hee's drunk.
>
> *Franck.*   If so
> Faith I would marry him; My friends I hope
> Would make him drink.
>
> (5.2.636)

The next step is to overcome his reluctance to face Franck. This is accomplished with Clora's suggestion:

> *Clora.*   Wee'le anger him I warrant ye,
> Let one of the maides take a good bowle of water,
> Or say it be a piss-pott, and power't on's head.
>
> (5.2.638)

(Fletcher always prefers "ye" to "you".) The stratagem works and Jacomo is brought into the house: "Pisse on my head? for surely it was pisse" (5.3.640). The lovers are united and join all the marriages at the end of the play.

Jacomo's thin legs suggest casting for a specific actor. It could be an adult in a boys' company or a later revision for a mature actor in the King's Men, possibly for the "hungry knave" who appears in later plays. A comic actor could have fun with Jacomo.

Lelia is also a good role; like Bacha, it is a study in perverse wickedness. Her beauty, lust, and villainy combine to make her a near demoness, ready to lure men to their destruction. We first see her at her most unfilial, recalling and outdoing Lear's daughters, by rejecting her poor old father's plea for help:

> Father. I gave up all my state to make yours thus.
>
> Lelia.   'Twas as ye ought to do, and now ye cry for't
>   As children do for babies backe againe.
>
> Father. How wouldst thou have me live?
>
> Lelia.   I would not have ye,
>   Nor know no reason Father's should desire
>   To live, and be a trouble; when children
>   Are able to inherit, let them dye;
>   'Tis fit and lookt for, that they should do so.
>   (1.3.562)

If we have any doubt that we are in the world of *King Lear*, Lelia's instructions to her father—"Be any thing but old, and beggarly" (1.3.563)—should convince us.

Like Edmund, Goneril, and Regan, Lelia's goddess is nature, a nature of the self unchecked by the restraints of civilization and humanity. Oddly enough, however, when Julio, one of the men she has allured, comes to court her, he incurs her wrath by refusing to marry her; she is a demon-whore with a certain respect for the proprieties. When Angilo comes to help his friend Julio resist Lelia's wiles, he too is entrapped by her beauty—"From this hour / I heartily despise all honest women" (3.4.603)—but he is at first shocked when Julio agrees to marry Lelia. His attitude wavers but most significant is his expression of the view:

> I see no reason we should be confin'd
> In our affections; when all creatures else
> Enjoy stil where they like.
>   (3.4.604)

This naturalistic libertine argument so reminiscent of John Donne in poems like "Community" and "Confined Love" is the basis for the much attacked scene, admittedly hard to defend, when Lelia attempts to seduce her father.

The old man, after Lelia's rebuff, has been fitted out with new clothes by Jacomo and a fellow soldier who pity his sufferings. In one of those easy and comfortable stage conventions, Lelia does not recognize the transformed old gentleman as her father. Instead, the old fellow strikes her fancy or, more properly, her appetite. She sends her servant to fetch the old man to the house where he finds a small collation of delicacies and music.

The scene is carefully arranged to obtain the maximum surprising turns. Angilo, one of the gentlemen infatuated by Lelia, has bribed a maid to give him access to the house so that he may secretly admire Lelia's beauty. He is stationed in the playing area above the main stage and is a visible observer of the action. Lelia enters with her maid *"with a Night-gowne and Slippers,"* settles her father in a chair, offers him wine, and proceeds with her seduction:

> fall to your banquet Sir,
> And let us grow in mirth; though I am set
> Now thus far off you, yet four glasses hence
> I will sit here, and try, till both our bloods
> Shoote up and downe to finde a passage out,
> Then mouth to mouth we will walke up to bed,
> And undresse one another as we goe;
> Where both my treasure, body, and my soule
> Are your's to be dispos'd of.
>
> (4.4.625)

The old man, preserving the secret of his identity, replies only "Umh, umh" and, as the stage direction says, *"Makes signes of his white head and beard"* (4.4.626). We cannot be certain whether this was played more for the shock effect of Lelia's disgusting perversion or for the laughter, but the broad (if perverse) comic possibilities are certainly not absent. Lelia reassures him that age is no bar and that she hopes to learn "something in the way of lust / I may be better for" and boasts:

> But I can teach
> These young ones; but this day I did refuse
> A paire of 'em, *Julio,* and *Angilo,*
> And told them they were as they were,
> Raw fooles and whelps.

The stage direction adjacent to this passage is "Angilo *makes discontented signes*" (4.4.626). It is hard to imagine that this moment did not draw a laugh from the audience, reducing the prurience.

One turn accomplished, Fletcher gives us another when the father reveals his identity to Lelia, who calmly declares her lust unabated and claims she recognized him all along, that when she turned him out of the house she was testing his "carriage in calamity" and that he behaved so nobly "That I have turn'd the reverence of a childe / Into the hot affection of a Lover" (4.4.627). She continues with unabated sangfroid to his shock and horror at her incestuous advances with a naturalistic argument that " 'tis not against nature / For us to lye together":

> 'Tis our generall nature
> To procreate, as fires is to consume,
> And it will trouble you to finde a sticke
> The fire will turne from. If't be natures will
> We should not mixe, she will discover to us
> Some apparent crosseness, as our organs
> Will not fit. . . .
>
> (4.4.628)

The argument recalls Donne's "Progesse of the Soule": "Men, till they tooke laws which made freedom lesse, / Their daughters, and their sisters did ingresse."[17]

The father, of course, is not won by his daughter's casuistry; instead, he draws his sword and threatens to kill her and himself. This is the time for another turn in the scene; Angilo reveals himself from his perch above. He prevents the murder and the suicide and with much kicking and screaming bustles Lelia off to a place where she may consider her sins and learn repentance. She repents and is married to one of the fops at the end of the play.

The scene is not especially edifying, but that it is "disgustingly prurient" is open to question. There is no question that it is highly theatrical and constructed for the most striking and melodramatic effects. That Fletcher was concerned with the moral content of the scene beyond its capability to shock is doubtful. Moreover, the possibilities for laughter are inescapable, and laughter would greatly modify the tone. So too would the tone be changed if both Lelia and her father were played by boys. The little-old-man-boy and the wicked-enchantress-boy make the scene considerably more ludicrous than lubricious. Nonetheless, the comedy is hardly wholesome.

Lelia's offstage repentance has annoyed a number of critics. William Appleton found it "cynical and perfunctory" and concluded that "as a creation she fails, for we are invited to consider her both as a satirical portrait of a lecherous woman and also as a romantic heroine."[18] Pearse also objects to Lelia's offstage reform and conversion but disagrees with Appleton's view of Lelia as satiric and romantic. Instead, she argues that "Lelia is presented as a moral exemplum" and that "*The Captain* is like Elizabethan moral literature in emphasizing the allurements of a courtesan in order to warn of the danger she presents." But offstage or not, Lelia does repent and she really does not present much of a danger. The young men buzzing about her are quite unhurt and the gull who is tricked into marrying her is perfectly happy after being assured that she has plenty of money:

> So I may have the meanes
> I doe not much care what the woman is:
> Come my sweet heart, as long as I shall finde
> Thy kisses sweet, and thy meanes plentifull,
> Let people talke their tongues out.
>
> (5.5.649)

The Captain is a weak play because it is not sufficiently coherent or consistent in its point of view. The Jacomo-Franck plot and the Lelia plot are not well joined. But the sense that they do not get on may stem from the critical tendency to read Lelia as more serious than she really is and to look for a greater tragicomic texture in her and her plot than is really there. The Lelia plot with its themes of naturalistic libertinism strives to shock and to convey the same sense of rakehell naughtiness found in Donne's early work. The play speaks to the witty men at the Inns of Court who delight in paradoxes and problems such as "A Defence of Women's Inconstancy" or "That Nature is Our Worst Guide." There is something to be said for the play that its most outrageous scene can still annoy.

The Scornful Lady by Beaumont and Fletcher is a far better written play, structurally and stylistically more sophisticated, if tamer, than *The Captain*. It achieved considerable popularity after the Restoration and became part of the repertory. Between 1616 and 1711 it was published in eleven quarto editions. It was written between 1610 and 1616, but likely around 1610. The title page of the 1616 quarto edition describes it as "Acted . . . by the Children of Her Majesty's Revels."[19] M. C. Bradbrook's description of Fletcher's comic practice in general is thoroughly applicable to *The Scornful Lady:* "In Fletcher's world no serious issues should be allowed to intrude: his plays are in a holiday mood, and the fantasy of the story is matched by the fragile, indirect motives of the characters. They may be allowed a generous impulse or a freakish whim: very rarely are they permitted to drop the mask or pause in the gay galliard."[20] The two plots of the play, a duel of the sexes and a story of a prodigal younger brother, are the occasion for high jinks, high spirits, and some lively language.

The plots are neatly fused and the play as a whole well constructed. The scornful lady of the title, throughout the play called only the Lady, punishes her lover, the Elder Lovelesse, with a year's exile abroad because he has presumed to kiss her in public. The duel of the sexes is thus joined. Lovelesse's younger brother has squandered his own inheritance and lost everything to the usurer Moorecraft. Nonetheless, with the exquisite bad judgment frequent in comedy, the Elder Lovelesse leaves his brother in charge of his house with an allowance of three hundred pounds under the loosest supervision of the old steward Savill. Young Lovelesse predictably invites his cronies, a Captaine, a Traveller, a Poet, and a Tobacco-man (a smoker, not a merchant), to share his good fortune. They quickly agree to spend the money in the wisest way: "wee'l have it all in drinke, let meate and lodging goe, th'are transitory, and shew men meerely mortall: then wee'l have wenches, every one his wench, and every weeke a fresh one: weele keep no powderd fleshe [preserved meat]: all these we have by warrant under the Title of things necessarie" (*DW,* vol. 2; 1.2.477).

Fletcher's control of language here is brilliant. It is the very speaking voice of the Jacobean stage gentleman. It defines the action to come and is so succinct that the plot with the Younger Lovelesse hardly needs more summary. He will, of course, corrupt the steward, sell the property for ready cash to the usurer, buy a knighthood, and with his knighthood win the rich widow.

The overplot of the Elder Lovelesse and the Lady, however, goes through a variety of turns and counterturns before it is resolved. Lovelesse, worried that the Lady will entertain another suitor—she does; his name is Welford—returns in disguise. To trick the Lady into declaring her love he tells her that Lovelesse was washed overboard and drowned. The Lady betrays her love for Lovelesse, but Lovelesse unconsciously reveals himself to her. She now plays her

trick by summoning Welford and declaring that she will give him
the love she should have given Lovelesse. This forces Lovelesse to
declare his identity, at which point the Lady claims she knew him
all along and sends him and Welford both away. The return of
Elder Lovelesse also neatly dovetails into the plot of his scapegrace
younger brother. When the Elder Lovelesse in a nicely comic scene
informs his brother of his own death, Young Lovelesse receives the
news with the greatest cheerfulness:

> Fill him some wine. Thou dost not see me moov'd,
> These transitory toyes nere trouble me,
> Hee's in a better place, my friend, I know't.
> ....
> Nay, let's all beare it well, wipe, *Savill,* wipe,
> Teares are but throwne away:
> We shall have wenches now, shall we not, *Savill?*
> (2.2.486)

In short order he purchases the knighthood that will win him the
widow and sells the estate to the usurer Moorecraft.

It is now time for Lovelesse's counterturn against the Lady. He
boasts that he is completely cured of his love for her, but once more
the Lady defeats him by feigning a faint that draws from him a
protestation of his real feelings for her. His expression of love produces more mockery from the Lady. For the final turn in the love
duel he joins forces with his sometime rival Welford, who disguises
himself as a woman and masquerades as Lovelesse's betrothed.

This bit of foolery is doubly successful. The Lady claims Lovelesse
on grounds of his earlier promises and her sister, Martha, is so sorry
for the rejected "betrothed" that she asks "her" to stay the night:

> *Martha.* Your bed shal be no worse then mine; I wish
> I could but doe you right.
> *Welford.* My humble thankes:
> God grant I may live to quit your love.
> (5.2.537)

An additional advantage of this somewhat antique joke is that it
can be milked for another laugh the next morning when Martha
has discovered her error. Perhaps the humor is pushed still farther

by the boy actor playing a man pretending to be a woman. There is also comic satisfaction in the inevitability of the solution. The camera lingers lovingly on the banana before the pratfall. The audience knows the joke and expects the mechanics of the disguise and the bedtrick, shares the triumph of the perpetrators, and delights in the foreknowledge of the absolute certainty of the resolution. A good deal of the strength of *The Scornful Lady* is just in the way the authors keep the comic ball bouncing with a comfortable sort of traditional ingenuity.

Young Lovelesse marries the widow. Elder Lovelesse marries the Lady. Welford marries Martha. A fourth marriage is made by another couple as yet unmentioned. They are the clowns, the curate Roger and the Lady's old waiting gentlewoman Abigail. Their romance is interrupted when Abigail is taken with Welford and coquettishly drops her glove and flirts with him, much to his disgust: "This is the strangest pamperd peece of flesh towards fiftie, that ever frailty cop't withall, what a trim *Lenvoy* heere she has put upon me: these woemen are a proud kinde of cattell, and love this whoreson doing so directly, that they wil not sticke to make their very skinnes Bawdes to their flesh" (3.1.493). Roger is the butt of the facetious humor of the gentleman, some of it directed at his clerical status and his language, some at his position in the household, so equivocal that he is often sent on errands. These upper servants suggest the great house world of *Twelfth Night*. In the inexorable drive toward marriage only the usurer Moorecraft is left single, but he is converted to generosity and beyond: "He's turn'd Gallant. . . . / . . . and is now called, *Cutting Moorecraft*" (5.4.543).

It is not difficult to understand the popularity of *The Scornful Lady*. The plots, that of the reluctant lady to be tamed to matrimony and the prodigal younger brother, were popular and familiar in themselves. Both situations promise inevitable comic harmonies. A major pleasure in watching a play built on these commonplace premises is in being aware of the playwright's technique, of seeing just how the banana is placed and how the inevitable fall is angled. The authors of *The Scornful Lady* demonstrate considerable skill in the plotting. The characters in the play are equally familiar and provide some good roles, especially Abigail, Roger, and the wastrel Young Lovelesse. *The Scornful Lady* is not as interesting a play as *The Captain,* but it is more polished than any of the early plays and shows a firm control of theatrical conventions.

With the exception of *The Faithful Shepherdess*, the early plays we have looked at all show a strong sense of what the audience wanted. *The Faithful Shepherdess* is singular in its uncompromising sense of what the genre and the artistic intentions of the playwright demanded. Whatever speculation we can make about the private theaters, the boys' companies, and their audiences, and about whatever changes may have occurred in the makeup of the audience when the King's Men took over Blackfriars Theater, the early plays for the boys and for the private theater show a keen awareness of the audience and of what will work and please on the stage. These plays, moreover, use the fundamental themes, techniques, character types, and language that will characterize Fletcher's work throughout his career.

Chapter Three
"Love, Griefe, and Mirth": The Tragicomedies

If John Fletcher's personal dramatic genius was for comedy, his reputation and influence were greatest in tragicomedy. While the mode and some of its background have already been introduced in our discussion of *The Faithful Shepherdess,* the importance of Fletcher's tragicomedy cannot be overstated. However difficult acceptance and enjoyment of Fletcherian tragicomedy may be for contemporary readers, for the seventeenth-century theatergoer it was the dominant form. Arthur C. Kirsch, referring to Beaumont and Fletcher, put the matter succinctly and emphatically: "The characteristics of the tragicomic form they crystallized eventually acquired canonical status for all drama. Both the theatrical criticism and the plays of the later Jacobean and the Caroline periods are thoroughly subsumed by their dramaturgical principles. . . . No English dramatists before or since have had so extraordinary an influence."[1]

That Fletcher's plays were ever advantageously compared with those of Shakespeare and Jonson is difficult to imagine in the twentieth century, and the tragicomedies may seem especially remote. Yet tragicomedy itself is certainly a familiar modern dramatic form, perhaps the major modern dramatic genre. Moreover, our times are not immune to the uncertainties or the confusion of values many critics find in Beaumont and Fletcher. Certainly portions of John F. Danby's description of what he calls the Beaumont hero and we prefer to call the Fletcherian hero sounds contemporaneous: "He is cut off from the social past and the neighborly present and his future includes only death. He is absolved from the need to exert rational control, and incapable of compromise. He is self-enclosed in the splintering world of the contending absolutes, and all the violence of activity these call out can only end in self-destruction."[2] It does not seem farfetched to say that with an adjustment here and there the description aptly fits the characters in plays of Samuel Beckett and Harold Pinter.

But such a view needs to be qualified by the recognition that with Fletcher we are dealing with a professional playwright for the most successful commercial acting company in England. Neil Simon is closer to the mark than Beckett or Pinter. It is helpful to recall Robert Ornstein's view that Fletcher represents not a radical transformation of dramatic taste and style but "instead the final stage of a long-continuing evolution that transformed the drama from an amateur communal undertaking in provincial cities and towns into a capitalistic enterprise, a very skilled professional and commercial entertainment centered in the metropolis of London and influenced to varying degrees by the taste and patronage of the court."[3] Fletcher's shade would undoubtedly find Broadway and the television and film studios of Hollywood congenial. His commercialism is surely another shared interest.

Two more quotations will serve to round out this attempt to establish points at which the modern reader can comfortably approach Fletcher's plays and in particular his tragicomedies. Philip Edwards deftly summarizes the controlling elements of Fletcherian tragicomedy: "They are mystification, debate and persuasion, prurience, improbable plots with elaborate complications, strong scenes."[4] With the exception of "debate and persuasion" the description would fit most popular television series today. Edwards goes on to avouch the reality of the bugaboo that so disturbed critics in the nineteenth century and over which a surprising amount of ink has been spilled in the twentieth: "His plays are sexy plays. . . . Prurience is a fact in Fletcher. He is a moral writer with highly immoral tendencies." This is another way in which the modern reader can find comfortable familiarity in the successor to Shakespeare at the King's Men.

If there are many points of contact with Fletcher's dramaturgy, there are undeniable problems of reading and appreciation as well. Even if improbable plots are abundant in modern dramatic productions, Fletcher's improbable plots often outdo the possibilities of improbability. His characters are not presented in any convincing depth. Almost without exception they are not individuals but types. He is not interested in the development and revelation of character in a Shakespearean sense. Modern tragicomedy focuses most on the tragic or on the mixture of the tragic and comic. For Fletcher the comic aspect, the movement to the happy ending, the assertion of the positive resolution is most important. Action is organized around emotion and the broad expression of abstract ideals—honor, loyalty, nobility, chastity, and their antitheses. The presentation is scenic rather than developmental. Fletcher's dramatic practice does not yield to questions such as, "Discuss the development of X's character and how it relates to the conclusion of the last act." The appropriate questions for Fletcher are more likely to be, "How does the language and action of the scene illustrate the concept of loyalty to the prince?" or more simply, "What emotions does the scene evoke and play on?" and certainly, "How does wit operate in the scene?"

Perhaps the greatest difficulty for a modern audience is in Fletcher's use of the literary conventions of his day. J. F. Danby locates Fletcher at the end of the Sidneian tradition of a culture centered around the Great House, the stately homes of the aristocracy, linking him with the heroic and pastoral romance and with the poetry of the sonneteers and the metaphysicals. "The main poetic feature of Beaumont and Fletcher," he writes, "is their adaptation to the stage of the sonneteer's 'conceit.' The primary affiliation of their drama is with the Sidneians and the metaphysicals."[5] This useful approach is one way of addressing the puzzles presented by the tragicomedies, in particular, the question of how seriously and how literally a play is to be read.

Dramatic Conceits:
Philaster and *A King and No King*

Philaster was written jointly by Beaumont and Fletcher for the King's Men between 1608 and 1610. The title page of the first quarto edition published in 1620 indicates it was acted at the Globe. Although its style and form suggest the private theater, it lacks both the music and spectacle associated with the Blackfriars. It was an immediate success and, along with *The Maid's Tragedy* and *A King and No King*, established Fletcher and Beaumont as no longer apprentices, but as leading playwrights. The audience for tragicomedy Fletcher sought with *The Faithful Shepherdess* was found with *Philaster*. Or perhaps it is more accurate to say that in *Philaster* Fletcher achieved the popular tragicomic voice he missed in *The Faithful Shepherdess*. In *Philaster* there are woods to be lost in, extremes of emotion, surprise, turns and counterturns in the action, but no magic well, no Satyr, no fairyland; Spenser has been banished from Sidney's Arcadia. In *Philaster* the Sidneian materials from *Cu-*

pid's Revenge are readjusted, turned into romance, and transported to a Sicilian court not far from Whitehall and the politics of the England of King James I.

An usurper known only as "King" sits on the dual thrones of Sicily and Calabria. The rightful heir to the throne of Sicily, Philaster, a melancholy Sicilian—one of the many parallels and analogues with *Hamlet*—is beloved by the King's daughter, Arathusa. But as the King explains in an opening speech, which in its pompous measures recalls that of Claudius in *Hamlet*, he has betrothed Arathusa to Pharamond, a Spanish prince, whom he also declares his heir.

Philaster blusters to Pharamond: "(O, I had a father / Whose memory I bow to). . . . I tell thee, *Pharamond*, / When thou art King, looke I be dead and rotten . . ." (*DW*, vol. 1; 1.1.404) and so draws the King's rebuke in another *Hamlet*-like exchange:

> *King.*　　　　　　　Sure hee's posest.
> *Philaster.* Yes, with my father's spirit: It's here, O King,
> 　　A dangerous spirit: now he tells me King,
> 　　I was a Kings Heire, bids me be a King,
> 　　And whispers to me, these are all my subjects:
> 　　Tis strange, he will not let me sleepe, but dives
> 　　Into my fancy, and there gives me shapes,
> 　　That kneele, and doe me service, cry me King:
> 　　But I'le suppresse him, he's a factious spirit,
> 　　And will undoe me:—[*to Pharamond*] noble sir, your hand,
> 　　I am your servant.
>
> *King.*　　　　　　　Away, I do not like this:
> 　　I'le make you tamer, or I'le dispossesse you
> 　　Both of life and spirit: for this time
> 　　I pardon your wild speech, without so much
> 　　As your imprisonment.

(1.1.407)

We may note in passing the assured quality of the verse, the biting effect of Philaster's repetition of "King." The dramatic moment is intense and the political issue is sharply defined; Lord Dion amplifies its complexity by his comment that the King dare not imprison Philaster because of his popularity with the people. Philaster's turbulent psychological state is established, and after the King's exit the loyalty of the courtiers to Philaster is made clear.

Philaster, indeed, seeks to divert Dion from his full expression
of willingness to support a rebellion by a polite question in a few
apparently throw-away lines:

> *Philaster.*   My Lord *Dion,*
> You had a vertuous Gentlewoman, cald you father,
> Is she yet alive?
>
> *Dion.*   Most honor'd sir, she is:
> And for the penance but of an idle dreame,
> Has undertooke a tedious pilgrimage.
>
> (1.1.408)

This apparently trifling exchange is the introduction (or perhaps
lack of introduction) of one of the major characters in the play.
Dion's daughter, Euphrasia, is not in fact on a pilgrimage but,
hopelessly in love with Philaster, she has disguised herself as a boy
and become Philaster's page, Bellario. To the more acute members
of the audience the lines must have provided enough mystification
to suggest a clue to be stored and watched just as a seemingly trivial
remark will alert the audience in a mystery.

The political situation is complicated by the joint loves of Arathusa and Philaster. He will learn of her love in a way that will
begin with mystification for both him and the audience. Despite
the cautionary remarks of the courtiers, Philaster accepts Arathusa's
summons. The scene exemplifies Fletcher's delight in emotional
complexity and in the witty play with what is said and what is
understood. Arathusa intends to tell Philaster that she loves him,
a socially awkward and difficult task for any Renaissance gentlewoman, let alone a princess. Her speech is at first extremely inept
and open to obvious misinterpretation:

> *Arathusa.*   *Philaster,* know,
> I must enjoy these Kingdomes.
>
> *Philaster.*   Madam, both?
>
> *Arathusa.* Both, or I dye: by heaven I die *Philaster,*
> If I not calmely may enjoy them both.
>
> *Philaster.* I would doe much to save that noble life;
> Yet would be loth to have posterity
> Finde in our stories, that *Philaster* gave
> His right unto a Scepter, and a Crowne,
> To save a Ladies longing.

Arathusa.   Nay then heare:
     I must, and will have them, and more—

Philaster.   What more?

Arathusa. Or loose that little life the gods prepared,
     To trouble this poore peece of earth withall.

Philaster. Madam, what more?

Arathusa.   Turne then away thy face.

Philaster. No.

Arathusa. Doe.

Philaster. I can indure it: turne away my face?
     I never yet saw enemy that lookt
     So dreadfully, but that I thought my selfe
     As great a Basaliske as he; or spake
     So horrible, but that I thought my tongue
     Bore thunder underneath, as much as his:
     Nor beast that I could turne from: shall I then
     Beginne to feare sweete sounds? a Ladies voyce,
     Whom I doe love? Say you would have my life,
     Why, I will give it you; for it is of me
     A thing so loath'd, and unto you that aske,
     Of so poore use, that I shall make no price:
     If you intreate, I will unmov'dly heare.

Arathusa. Yet for my sake a little bend thy lookes.

Philaster. I doe.

Arathusa.   Then know I must have them, and thee.

Philaster. And me?

Arathusa.   Thy love: without which, all the Land
     Discovered yet, will serve me for no use,
     But to be buried in.

Philaster.   Ist possible?

            (1.2.411–12)

The exchange has been quoted at such length because it so clearly illustrates how narrative interest is surpassed by the emotional and rhetorical concerns of the dramatic moment and its language. The interest is in the dance of misunderstanding and misspeaking that keeps the exchange taut and gives surprise to an expression of mutual love that can hardly be surprising to an alert audience.

The conventions of romance demand that Princess Arathusa love

Prince Philaster and he her. The dramatist must create the emotion
of surprise by clever manipulation. Arathusa's modesty results in
her inept and easily misunderstood approach. Philaster appears at
first incredulous—"Madam, both?"—and then wittily ironic: "To
save a Ladies longing." When Arathusa asks him to turn away his
face, he misreads again and blusters, but in the bluster is his own
declaration of love. The movement ends with Philaster's wondrous
"Ist possible?" The Prince who expected the worst has heard the
best; instead of the demands of an imperious and greedy princess
that he surrender his royal rights, he has heard a declaration of love
and the suggestion that he will regain his rights. To find Philaster
obtuse and the scene unrealistic is like complaining of the unnatural
formality of the minuet.

The lovers agree to communicate through Philaster's page, Bellario, who will go to serve Arathusa, and the next link in the
developing complication is forged. Philaster describes his finding
Bellario weeping by the side of a fountain, a freshly woven garland
of flowers by him, in tones so redolent of the romance tradition
that the audience must have been sure that this page was the inevitable girl in disguise. The arrival of the Spanish prince, Pharamond, raises tension, but a serious quarrel between the two rivals
is avoided. After Philaster's grumpy exit the tone of the scene
undergoes yet another change:

> *Pharamond.* Tis an odd fellow Madam, we must stop
> His mouth with some office, when we are married.
>
> *Arathusa.* You were best to make him your controwler.
>
> (1.2.416)

Arathusa's witty pun floats past Pharamond, but his suggestion for
a moment returns us to the world of court politics.

Still another shift occurs when Pharamond reveals the purpose of
his visit; he proposes that Arathusa sleep with him before the wedding. When she indignantly withdraws, Pharamond is left to close
the act with a farcical moan: "The constitution of my body will
never hold out till the wedding: I must seek else-where" (1.2.416).
It is a fine comic moment that sets up what will be a major turn
in the plot. The King's plan for the marriage of Arathusa and
Pharamond will be foiled because the randy Spaniard does seek
elsewhere.

The act is a superlative example of the Fletcherian style. It opens with an evocation of Hamlet's world—the corrupt court, usurpation and resistance to the usurpation, a hero in a complex and difficult time, a love clouded by politics and misunderstanding; into this brooding setting romance conventions are introduced—the page who will be a go-between weeping by a fountain; and finally a note of bawdy comedy and satirical handling of the ridiculous Spaniard, a figure of jingoistic fun and topical concern.

Pharamond sets out to ease his lust: "I was never so long without sport in my life, and in my conscience, tis not my fault. O, for our countrey ladies!" (2.2.418) and quickly finds his match in the lustful court lady, Megra. Their plans for an assignation, however, are overheard by Galatea, hiding behind a curtain. Acting on her information, the furious King confronts the guilty pair. Megra, not put to rout, laughs and counterattacks by accusing Arathusa of making love with her page:

> Urge me no more, I know her, and her haunts,
> Her layes, her leaps, and outlayes, and will discover all;
> Nay, will dishonor her. I know the boy
> She keepes, a handsome boy: about eighteene:
> Know what she does with him, where, and when.
>
> (2.4.430)

Turn and counterturn. Since this is the world of tragicomic romance the King and his courtiers are easily persuaded of the vice of the innocent Arathusa. In a rich irony Dion in particular is willing to assume Arathusa's guilt with the "smooth boy." He sees, moreover, political opportunity in the charge. If Philaster is willing to believe the accusation against Arathusa, he will be willing to revolt against the King to regain his title. To convince Philaster of Arathusa's guilt Dion plays Iago to Philaster's Othello, even going a step beyond Iago by swearing that he saw them in the act. The irony is double. Dion is unknowingly accusing his own daughter (and of an impossibility), and in lying for a good cause he brings her life into danger. The drama of the moment is in the complex ironies, in the exercise of wit, in the ingenuity of the conceit.

That ingenuity is pushed still farther when Philaster, demanding that Bellario confess his/her guilt, draws his sword and threatens to kill him/her. Bellario's response would fit easily in a poem by that most extravagantly conceited of poets Richard Crashaw:

> Hew me asunder, and whilst I can thinke, [*Kneeles.*]
> I'le love those pieces you have cut away,
> Better then those that grow: and kisse those limbes,
> Because you made um so.
>
> (3.1.439)

The audience's pleasure in the scene is certainly in the extremes of emotion but equally in the literary wit of the language and circumstances. Of course, full enjoyment necessitates the audience's awareness that the page is no page but a lovelorn girl.

The fourth act brings the characters together in the forest where the King and court have come to hunt. Bellario, dismissed by Philaster, is wandering forlornly about, weak, sad, and hungry, while Princess Arathusa has managed to get lost. The King's reaction to her disappearance—

> . . . I am your King,
> I wish to see my daughter, show her me!
> I do command you all, as you are subjects,
> To show her me! What, am I not your King?
> If ay, then am I not to be obeyed?

and Dion's response, "Yes, if you command things possible, and honest" (4.4.452)—have been cited as refutation of Coleridge's charge that Beaumont and Fletcher were "the most servile *jure divino* Royalists" and as a satire on King James's views on the nature of kingship.[6]

When Arathusa and Philaster meet in the forest they play one of the most famous and popular scenes in the Fletcherian canon. The fainting Arathusa encounters the wandering Bellario who takes her in his/her arms. When Philaster comes upon them, this sight, a confirmation of his fears, throws him into a mad rage, and he offers Arathusa his sword to kill him: "Then you and this your boy may live and reign / In lust without control" (4.5.455). He sends Bellario away and prepares to kill Arathusa, when a Country Fellow hoping to see the King chances on the shocking scene. Philaster wounds Arathusa and the Country Fellow rushes forward with a great cry of "Hold dastard, strike a woman!" (4.5.457).

This yawningly conventional bit of melodrama is turned into a brilliant theatrical moment by the astounding responses of Philaster and Arathusa to Country Gentleman's heroics. Philaster is all gracious gentility—"Leave us good friend"—while Arathusa cannot hide her aristocratic annoyance: "What ill-bred man art thou, to intrude thy selfe / Upon our private sports, our recreations?"

Small wonder the scene is depicted as the frontispiece of the 1620 quarto of *Philaster* and forms as well the subtitle of the play, *Love Lies a-bleeding*. The popularity of such a scene, its triumphant theatricality, is not far to seek. The cliché of the melodramatic rescue by a noble citizen is allowed to appear and then turned upside down. Conventional expectations are not only unsatisfied but there is a temporary pause in the drama in which aristocratic solidarity is asserted and in which we are reminded of the playfulness of the play and the tragicomic nature of this world is reinforced. The strength of the scene is in its daring wittiness and the theatrical and social joke it makes.

But of course the action and excitement of the play does not stop so that the witty conceit of the scene may be admired, but rushes on with more twists and turns. Philaster is wounded by the Country Fellow and runs off. He comes upon the sleeping Bellario and in his madness stabs her, but then falls himself of his wounds. He asks Bellario to kill him, admitting he stabbed the Princess; Bellario, of course, refuses, and when Dion and the other courtiers arrive, he/she claims that it is she who has wounded Arathusa. Philaster then crawls out of a bush to defend Bellario's innocence and admits his crime.

He is imprisoned and condemned to death. In prison he comes to himself and recognizes the love and truth of both Arathusa and Bellario. The marriage of Arathusa and Philaster takes place offstage, but is announced by Bellario as Hymen in a masquelike scene. The King immediately declares he will execute Arathusa, too, but now the heroic citizens, clearly trueborn Englishmen all, the traditional noble citizens of the popular stage, seize Pharamond, rescue Philaster, and propose to overthrow the King. Philaster rejects the offer and has the citizen army return home. The King repents and reforms, accepts Philaster as his heir and his marriage with Arathusa and sends Pharamond back to Spain and orders Megra to go with him.

The last revelatory turn remains, however. Megra revives her old accusation against Arathusa and Bellario. When the King orders Bellario stripped for torture, she is forced to reveal her identity to Dion, who had been in the forefront of hauling her away to torture. Filled with shame he recognizes the daughter he had slandered and

brought to such risk. Bellario/Euphrasia rejects Philaster's offer to
find her an appropriate husband and chooses to live with Philaster
and Arathusa, serving the Princess and chastely loving Philaster.
The King returns Philaster his Kingdom of Sicily and the inheritance
of Calabria and speaks the final harmonious lines:

> . . . Let Princes learne
> By this to rule the passions of their blood,
> For what Heaven wils can never be withstood.
>   (5.5.484)

One critic has described *Philaster* as "written in the middling
mood of pure recreation."[7] As such it was, in its day and considerably
beyond, a major success. The re-creation, however, is complex, and
the play addresses itself to audiences past and present in a variety
of ways. Philip J. Finkelpearl, for example, argues that the play is
a comedy rather than a tragicomedy and that Philaster is "a comic
fool in the tradition of many unsure husbands and lovers in Jacobean
drama who are obsessed by cuckoldry and live in a world of unceasing
cuckoo calls and sprouting horns."[8] Such an interpretation, ignoring
Philaster's madness and the function of the literary conceit in the
play, is more convincing from a twentieth-century perspective than
from that of the seventeenth, but such a reading would possibly
play on the stage and reinforces the variety to be found in the play.
Similar problems of interpretation have been raised with *A King
and No King,* a play based, as the title indicates, on an elaborately
developed and cleverly revealed paradox. Is it pure entertainment?
Is it a serious tragicomedy or closer to being a mockery of its own
form? Does it have any sort of moral purpose and, if it does, is that
purpose buried in the play's sensationalism?

A King and No King was written in 1611, a collaborative effort
of Beaumont and Fletcher with the greater portion attributed to
Beaumont, and first published in quarto in 1619. It was written
for the King's Men and acted by them at both the Globe and the
Blackfriars. Although Fletcher's hand in the play is relatively small,
the play deserves mention both as exemplifying the joint theatrical
success of the collaborators writing for the King's Men and as another
example of the conceit as the central feature in the design of the
play.

Arbaces, king of Iberia, has returned victorious from the wars in

Armenia with the king of Armenia, Tigranes, his prisoner. He plans to release Tigranes once he has arranged that king's marriage with his sister, Panthaea, whom he has not seen since her childhood. When he sees her, he falls wildly in love with her himself. The problem of the play, then, is to resolve the forbidden incestuous love by demonstrating that Arbaces is a king and no king, a brother and no brother.

As the play develops the audience is presented a series of contradictions or inconsistencies to puzzle over. The victorious Arbaces is a hero whose heroism is compromised by bombastic boastfulness and a generally mercurial nature. Arbaces, as the loyal and sensible General Mardonius puts it, "is vainglorious, and humble, and angrie, and patient, and merrie, and dull, and joyfull, and sorrowfull, in extreamities in an houre" (*DW*, vol. 2; 1.1.185). Arbaces, then, is anything but the model hero, to say nothing of a king.

The audience will find additional puzzlement in the news that the Iberian Queen Mother has been arrested *again* for plotting the assassination of Arbaces and still more puzzlement by the queen's response when Gobrius chides her for this exceedingly unmaternal behavior: "But *Gobrius* let us talke; you know this fault / Is not in me as in another woman" (2.1.202). Why is Gobrius, the audience will also wonder, so concerned that the normal dynastic marriage of state that Arbaces is arranging for his sister and King Tigranes not take place? Why should Gobrius assure Arbaces, speaking of Panthaea, that "You will be loath to part with such a jewell," thus provoking Arbaces's dumbfounded response: "To part with her, why *Gobrius* art thou mad? / Shee is my sister" (3.1.216)?

The answers are clear when, after many zigs and zags of the plot, it is revealed that Gobrius is Arbaces's father. The Queen, it develops, married the late king when he was very old. Anxious to produce an heir, but fearing that the king was too old to generate one, she feigned pregnancy and at the proper time took Gobrius's newborn son to raise as her own and as heir to the throne, an arrangement in which Gobrius was willing to participate to advance his son to the kingship. The old king, however, shortly before his death did father a child and rightful heir, Panthaea. Thus Arbaces is a king and no king, but marriage to Panthaea will make him one.

Arbaces's character faults, then, are not comments on absolute kings, or satire, or part of an overall comic texture, but clues. The character flaws are hints to an audience ready to unravel a puzzling paradox that he is no king. Until Gobrius's revelation and his legitimizing marriage with Panthaea, Arbaces is an usurper, albeit an unknowing one. He has the potential to be a true king, but his erratic and boastful behavior reveals that he is not. The movement of the tragicomic action is toward truth and legitimization.

The conceit of the play is in the extended paradox. The pattern and use of the conceit may be compared to many paintings of Fletcher's contemporary Peter Paul Rubens. The brilliant *Rape of the Daughters of Leucippus* (ca. 1619) provides a specific example. The painting depicts the immortals Castor and Pollux carrying off the rather massive and thoroughly unclothed daughters of Leucippus, a king of Messene. At first glance the scene is filled with violence, movement, and emotion. One brother is mounted on his horse, the other dismounted while his horse rears up in the background. The red cloak of one flares against the blue sky. The arms of the maidens reach imploringly to the sky; their bodies twist with the corkscrewing swirl of the lines of the painting.

A close look, however, reveals that the violence is not really very violent. The faces of Castor and Pollux are intent, but calm and determined, not violent. The maidens are large, lovely Rubens girls, all dimpled flesh, but Castor and Pollux are having no difficulty lifting these hefty lasses. Nor do the ladies appear to be resisting or seem deeply agitated. They have adopted a conventional bodily pose of dismay and surprise, but will almost float onto the horses and away with their abductors under a welcoming blue sky. On the far left a charming fat putto hangs on the bridle of one of the horses and smiles benignly out at the viewers.

The painting depicts a rape and no rape, a paradox of a holy rape. The conceit of the painting and of the play are similar and so is a part of the pleasure derived from both. This is not to disagree with the view that "The primary concern of their [Beaumont and Fletcher] kind of play is to order its material, not in terms of narrative form, but in terms of what might be called emotional or psychological form,"[9] but to emphasize that the emotional patterns are controlled by the central dramatic conceit.

The Rhetoric of the Improbable

The dramatic conceit can be found as central to almost all the tragicomedies in the Fletcher canon. However, there are numerous

other organizing principles. A choice of approach is inevitably somewhat arbitrary, as is any grouping or selection of plays to be discussed
from such a large number of works. A major organizing feature is
often the dramatic resolution of extravagant and improbable hypotheses. "What if there were a man or woman who . . ." and
then as bizarre and extreme a situation as possible is put. *The Mad
Lover,* a popular play written by Fletcher alone, probably in 1616,
asks just such a bizarre question: "What if a man, maddened by
love, offers a girl his heart and takes the conventional metaphor
literally?"

On such a flimsy grounding is *The Mad Lover* based. Memnon,
a bluff old general, a veteran of the camps of war and totally inexperienced with women, has returned victorious from the wars to
the city of Paphos, the city on the island of Cyprus associated with
Venus. At the first sight of Princess Calis he cries *"O Venus"* and,
stricken with love, *"He kneeles amaz'd, and forgets to speake"* (*DW*,
vol. 5: 1.1.17). Memnon's entrance had been victorious and full of
bombast. He boasted his familiarity with war and his innocence of
courtly manners. Now he moves quickly from mere rusticity to love
madness. When he clumsily informs Calis that he has a heart and
he wishes she held it in her hand, she teasingly replies, "Doe you
give it?" and promises to accept it:

> *Calis.* And you shall see I dare accept it Sir
> Tak't in my hand and view it: if I finde it
> A loving and a sweet heart as you call it,
> I am bound, I am—
>
> *Memnon.* No more, Ile send it to ye,
> As I have honour in me you shall have it.
>
> *Calis.* Hansomlye done Sir, and perfum'd by all meanes,
> The weathers warme Sir.
>
> (1.2.29)

The princess is having a delightful time mocking this unsophis-
ticated and dotty old general; Venus teases Mars. Memnon is dotty
indeed but deadly serious in his madness. In the unraveling of the
plot Fletcher varies straight comedy with court satire and tragicomic
romance. Three other lovers are included in the action—Chilax, a
bluff old officer who makes love to the "old wanton" who is the

priestess of Venus; Siphax, a soldier who has the audacity to fall in love with the princess; and finally Memnon's brother, Polidor.

When Siphax goes to the princess to plead for Memnon, he falls in love himself, and asks his sister, Cleanthe, who is one of Calis's waiting gentlewomen, to help him. She agrees to bribe the Priestess of Venus to give the princess a false oracle instructing her to marry the first man she sees when she comes out of the temple. Chilax overhears all this and arranges for Siphax's cast mistress, Cloe, to disguise herself as the princess. Thus Siphax is properly cheated of the princess and his presumption rewarded with an appropriate, if undesired, marriage.

Polidor's role is to effect his brother's cure and to marry the princess himself. His analysis of the basic cause of Memnon's madness is that it is "meerly heate" and he proposes attempting a cure with a good-looking whore dressed like the princess. Polidor also arranges for a curative masque to be played and sung by Orpheus and Charon, warning that suicides cannot enter Elysium. The treatment has a calming effect on Memnon. He is not taken in by the whore—"by heaven she stinkes" (4.5.77)—but he laughs and is gentle with the whore—"Alas poore whore, / Go, be a whore still, and stinke worse" (5.1.78)—thus demonstrating the efficacy of Polidor's psychotherapy.

When the King learns that Calis has fallen in love with Polidor, he offers her to him in marriage. Polidor, however, nobly refuses for Memnon's sake. Calis now visits the temple of Venus where Chilax is in robes pretending to be the oracle. A thunderclap drives him from the temple and Venus descends to declare to Calis, "A dead love thou shalt enjoy" (5.3.82). When Polidore, still working to win Calis for his brother, arranges his own mock funeral so Calis will marry Memnon, she says that she will die on his tomb instead. Memnon is so moved by Polidore's apparent sacrificial death that he declares he will follow Polidore to the grave. Polidore then reveals that he is not dead and so fulfills the oracle. When the King gives Calis to Polidore, he, exacting her promise to obey his will, gives her to Memnon. Memnon is so touched by his brother's generosity that he resigns all claims in Calis:

> I would resign all freely; 'tis all love
> To me, all marriage rites, the joy of issues,
> To know him fruitfull, that has been so faithfull.
>   (5.4.96)

Memnon is completely restored to sanity and self-knowledge: "My cold stiffe carkasse, would have frozen ye,— / Warres, warres." "Ye shall have warres" (5.4.97), the King assures him. Venus and Mars will not wed. Youth will have youth and Mars will have war. The improbability of the initial premise is answered; the metaphor remains a metaphor. We cannot dispose of hearts in goblets or cups, but the improbable hypothesis provides a happy romp over the stage.

The Queen of Corinth (1616–18) is a collaborative work in which the hands of Fletcher, Philip Massinger, and Nathan Field have been detected. Although *The Queen of Corinth* is clearly a potboiler, it is a very competently constructed entertainment and of interest to us here mainly for its complex and improbable plot, which hinges on the legal problems surrounding a double rape.

General Leonidas has returned to Corinth victorious, having concluded a peace with Agenor, the prince of Argos; and he has arranged the prince's marriage with his sister, Merione. The queen has agreed to the marriage in spite of Prince Theanor's previous honorable intentions towards Merione. That Theanor's apparent acceptance of the planned marriage is deceitful is clear from his first entrance, when we see him with his vicious adviser, Crates, examining the scene for the rape, "this night's action," in vaults so hollow and walls so thick "As Dian there might suffer violence" (*W,* vol. 6; 1.1.3).

In the course of the first act we encounter a set of fools who will satirize ignorant travelers and duellists and more importantly are introduced to Crates's younger brother, Euphanes, as noble a youth as Crates is base, and to Euphanes's love, the rich and generous Lady Beliza. The act, set the night before Merione's wedding, ends with Crates and others of Theanor's party carrying off Merione.

Act 2 (which has been attributed to Fletcher on the basis of linguistic analysis) opens with Merione's lament:

> To whom now shall I cry? What pow'r thus kneel to?
> And beg my ravisht honor back upon me?
> Deaf, deaf, you gods of goodness, deaf to me,
> Deaf Heaven to all my cries. . . .
>
> (2.1.17)

It is a fine rhetorical moment for the actor. After a little masquing scene in which *"Enter six disguis'd, singing and dancing to a horrid Musick, and sprinkling water on her face,"* Merione is drugged to sleep and deposited on her brother's doorstep.

The opportunities for full emotional exploitation are not missed when Merione is discovered, and upon awakening she is given the opportunity of expatiating once more upon her dishonor. The noble Agenor offers to marry her, but she vows to retire from the world and live a nun until her death. More foolery with the clowns allows an unstated amount of time to pass in which Euphanes has become the queen's favorite, a major power in the court, and thoroughly aroused Theanor's jealousy.

When the queen grants Euphanes permission to marry Beliza, Theanor pretends that he is no longer jealous, and his mother deputizes him to present Euphanes with her gift of jewels. Acting on the advice of Crates, Theanor slips Euphanes the ring he took from Merione when he raped her among the jewels.

Euphanes, of course, gives the ring to Beliza who naturally puts it on. Merione recognizes her ring and Euphanes is not simply suspected of rape, but virtually convicted of it by Leonidas and Agenor. They seize the fortress and hold Theanor for ransom, demanding that the queen surrender Euphanes to them for execution.

It is all highly improbable, if not downright silly, but it is managed with great dramatic skill. Before the discovery of Merione's ring we are given a little musical interlude in which Agenor, Leonidas, and Beliza attempt to comfort the poor lady. Two songs are sung to cheer her, *"A sad song," "Weep no more, nor sigh nor groan,"* and *"A lighter song,"* the therapeutic powers of which no doubt justified its doubtful propriety:

> Court Ladies laugh, and wonder. Here is one
> That weeps because her Maiden head is gone
> Whilst you do never frett, nor chafe, nor cry
> But when too long it keeps you company. . . .
> (3.2.45)

The scene, even with its easy acceptance of a moment of comedy, returns us to the grieving Merione and by so doing intensifies the drama of her discovery. It may even serve to accommodate in some measure the remarkable ease with which Agenor and Leonidas assume that the hitherto spotless Euphanes is guilty of rape.

Euphanes now offers himself unarmed to the rebels in exchange for the release of Theanor. Moreover, he convinces them of his innocence by reminding them of one of those little details so easily forgotten in the world of tragicomedy—he was with Leonidas at the time of the rape.

No doubt to save dramatic time and perhaps the effort of writing dialogue, the queen's forgiveness of Leonidas and Agenor is presented in dumb show. The problem now is to catch the rapist. In a key scene Conon fights with Crates. Euphanes stops the fight and shows such brotherly concern for the despicable Crates that nature triumphs and Crates is moved to virtue, brotherhood, and humanity. Crates reveals the truth of the old rape and plans for a new one.

The trap is now set for Theanor. He rapes Beliza (to annoy Euphanes) and is seized and brought to trial. The law concerning rape requires that the victim can ask either that her violator be compelled to marry her or be executed. Merione asks that Theanor marry her and Beliza asks for his death.

As Eugene M. Waith points out, this dilemma and other tricky problems like it used in other dramas, were drawn from the *Controversiae* of Seneca the Elder, declamations designed to train orators in the skills of debate.[10] *The Controversiae* contains exactly the problem put in *The Queen of Corinth*. Instead of extended debate, however, the trial scene is worked for its emotions. In spite of Merione's pleading, the queen orders Theanor's execution. Only then does Crates produce the final turn. Crates assisted Theanor in the rape of Merione because he believed a nuptial contract already existed and that she was therefore "his Wife before the face of Heaven" (4.3.61).

It may be objected that a precontract is only vaguely suggested at the start of the play and that there is no hint that Crates is anything other than a wicked assistant in a criminal rape. But more explicit information would have spoiled the scene and Crates's true view of rape is given when he tells Theanor, "To fall but once is manly, to persevere / Beastly, and desperate" (4.3.61). When Crates undergoes his conversion, he informs Euphanes of Theanor's intentions to rape Beliza and Merione is set in her place. The play ends with the reformation of Theanor and the standard rush to the altar. Theanor marries Merione; Euphanes weds Beliza; and the queen, not to be left, marries Agenor.

The substitute rape victim is a sensationalized variation on the popular bed-trick found in Shakespeare in both *All's Well That Ends Well* and *Measure for Measure*. Both Theanor and Crates (even granting the latter's moderate views on rape) are such consummate villains

that their conversions are totally unconvincing if we think of them
in a logical way. But logic is not a concern of *The Queen of Corinth*
or of Fletcherian tragicomedy in general; emotion is, and tragicomic
feeling. *The Queen of Corinth* is fast-moving, lively entertainment.
It appears lurid without really being so; its rapes are not really rapes;
its villains decent at bottom. A large portion of the kind of dramatic
satisfaction the play gives is in the cleverness of the windings and
turnings of the plot, in the naturalizing of the improbable.

The *Laws of Candy* (1619–23) has been described by G. E. Bentley
"as one of the least popular of the Fletcher plays—and deservedly
so," and as "a magnificent, Pirandellesque play" by Ian Fletcher.[11]
No matter how distant critical responses may be, it can easily be
agreed that the play is based on a set of improbable hypotheses the
source for which is again found in the Senecan *Controversiae*. Two
laws of Candy (Crete) state that the general judged the most heroic
in battle may demand a reward from the state and, much more
strangely, that ingratitude is punishable by death. The action of
the play begins with a paradox arising from the operation of the
first law and ends, after considerable sound and fury, with a happy
resolution coming from the unexpected and paradoxical application
of the second law.

The play opens, as do so many of Fletcher's plays, with a triumphant return home from war. Old General Cassilane demands the
reward of the state for his victory over the Venetians, but so does
his son, Antinous, newly launched on his military career. Here is
a basic conflict of father and son, the established old veteran and
the new hero. Each makes an address to the troops, one of those
stage moments appropriate to the oratorical origins of the *Controversiae* and to an audience of a time that still took pleasure in formal
rhetoric. Antinous makes his demand of the state. He asks the Senate
to erect a statue of his father inscribed "*Great* Cassilane, *Patron of
Candy's Peace,* / *Perpetual Triumpher*" (*W*, vol. 3; 1.2.248).

In another sort of dramatic world the play might end here; Cas-
silanes, however, is an unreasonable and cantankerous old man. His
son's filial piety is not such to him, but an insult. Cassilane now
retires, annoyed, to the country with his daughter Annophel. He
has been reduced to near poverty and had the bad judgment to allow
Gonzalo, a devious Venetian schemer who is plotting to take over
Candy and eventually Venice, to pay off his troops and has given

Gonzalo a mortgage for his land. Gonzalo provides the political subplot. It is difficult not to wonder if Fletcher's audience may not have seen in Gonzalo some hints of Count Gondomar, the long-term Spanish ambassador to England.

The beautiful and imperious Princess Erota is the center of the main romance material and links the father-son, political, and romantic plots. The role, that of the arrogant femme fatale, clearly one of the acting "lines" of the troop, has plenty of room for tearing passions to tatters. Erota rejects all lovers except for Antinous, who is not interested in her. However, he agrees to love her if she will get Cassilane out of Gonzalo's debt and power. She buys up Cassilane's mortgage from Gonzalo and rescues the old general from poverty. Gonzalo, moreover, has already been courting her so she has no difficulty in getting him to confess his wicked plots against Candy and Venice and his plan to make her queen.

Act 5 gathers all the characters together in the Senate House when Cassilane comes to demand the death penalty for Antinous on the grounds of ingratitude. Antinous, ever the loyal son, accepts the accusation and his guilt. The Senate has no choice but to accept his plea of guilty and condemns him to death. Erota, responding to this attack on Antinous, then charges Cassilane with ingratitude for her help. The Senate condemns him to death. This does not change Cassilane's mind, but it leads Antinous to charge Erota with ingratitude to him. He agreed to love her out of pity for her, but required that she would secretly assist her father. By making the assistance public and accusing Cassilane of ingratitude she is guilty of ingratitude to him. Erota, true and loving, confesses her guilt: " 'Las man, I meant not to outlive thy doom, / Shall we be friends in death?" (5.1.293). Once more the Senate has no choice but to condemn Erota to death.

Cassilane gloats over the perspective carnage: "I am dead / . . . and so is she and he, / We are all worms-meat now." Then Annophel steps forward and with a logic that surely can be called Pirandellesque charges the whole Senate with ingratitude for allowing the aged hero, defender of Candy, Cassilane, to fall into poverty. There is no possible resolution for such a dilemma but for Cassilane to repent and withdraw his accusation, Erota hers, Antinous his, and Annophel hers. The final steps to complete the dance is the arrest of Gonzalo and the marriages of Erota, in a sudden shift, to

Prince Philander of Cyprus who has been in love with her all along; and of Annophel to Fernando, a Venetian prisoner, a captive of Cassilane's.

None of the characters in *The Laws of Candy* really are of any interest; they are simply stock types. The plot is everything and everything in the plot depends on the improbabilities. If *The Laws of Candy* was not successful, the fault was not in the mechanics of the plot and the production of requisite turns and counterturns or in the use of the improbable. If anything, the mechanics work too well, the patterns are too formulaic, and when applied to basically uninteresting characters, the play fails to come to real life. Judged, however, as a transitory product for the demanding appetite of the London stage it is certainly a thoroughly polished piece of entertainment that exemplifies the use of the improbable as a source of plot design.

Extreme and exaggerated situations similar to those in the *Controversiae* are also dominant in *The Loyal Subject* (1618), but it is a more interesting and successful play. *The Loyal Subject*'s theme is honor, and its hero, old General Archas, is as obstinate in his maintenance of honor as old Cassilane is in his wrongheaded demand for recognition. But extreme and unyielding in his behavior as he is, Archas always retains his dignity.

Unlike *The Laws of Candy*, *The Loyal Subject* has been uniformly attributed to Fletcher alone and its superiority argues for *The Laws of Candy* as collaborative or revised. The action of *The Loyal Subject*, a series of variations on the theme of honor maintained through unswerving loyalty, is considerably more coherent and unified. The characters are also admittedly stock types, but lively, vigorous, and sometimes even realistic.

The basic story presumably came to Fletcher from an Italian novella by Bandello translated by William Painter in *The Palace of Pleasure* via Thomas Heywood's play *The Royal King and Loyal Subject*, written around 1600.[12] Heywood moved the setting from Persia to England; and Fletcher moved it to Moscow, at least in name, and altered details of plot and character.

Once more the play opens with the victorious return from the wars of an old general, a major role for a senior actor in the company, a role combining glimpses of past unchallenged power and the pathos of the encroachment of age and of power lost.

General Archas has been forced into retirement by the young

Duke of Moscow and refused a triumphal celebration for his victory. The young Duke's resentment stems from a public rebuke Archas gave him (at the request of the old Duke, his father) for improperly drilling the troops. The wicked Boroskie, interested only in his own advancement, keeps the Duke's resentment alive and encourages his mistreatment of Archas. In an emblematic scene Archas surrenders his armor, his colors, and his cased drums to the priests and vows never to fight again.

To the disgust of all the soldiers, Boroskie is made commander in chief; but when the Tartars rise up again and threaten Moscow, Boroskie feigns illness and retires to his bed. Archas takes up his arms and defeats the Tartars. Boroskie, however, maintains his influence over the Duke and counsels him not to meet Archas on his return, but to send him, unhonored, back into retirement again. The soldiers are so indignant at this insult that they refuse to collect their pay.

Archas bears the mistreatment honorably and loyally without a word of complaint. The Duke demands from Archas not only the treasure left in his care by the old Duke but his personal wealth as well, emblematically leaving him with just his old school gown and a volume of Seneca. The Duke delivers a final blow by ordering Archas to send his two beautiful young daughters, Honora and Viola, to the court where they will be subject to all its dangerous temptations. Archas accepts these indignities as well.

The scenes at court are some of the liveliest in the play. Archas's son Theodore escorts the girls to the court and drives off the sniffing courtiers with broad sarcasm, satirically offering the girls as sexual targets:

> They are fit for any thing.
> They'll wait upon a man, they are not bashfull,
> Carry his cloak, or untie his points, or any thing,
> Drink drunk, and take Tobacco; the familiarst fooles—
> This wench will leap over stools too, and sound a Trumpet,
> Wrastle, and pitch the Bar; they are finely brought up.
> *(DW,* vol. 5; 3.4.215)

His advice to his sisters is equally pungent, "Farewel wenches, keep close your ports, y'are washt else" (3.4.215). A good part of the life of *The Loyal Subject* derives from spirited comic language of this sort.

The girls are courted by the Duke, a courtship complicated by his ongoing courtship of Alinda, the beautiful servant to his sister Olympia. Alinda, to no one's surprise, is Archas, son of Archas, disguised as a girl and placed in the court by Putskie, alias Briskie, Archas's brother. Putskie has taken this step to insure that at least one son of Archas survives in case the Duke and Boroskie become more deadly.

When Archas is asked to dine at the court, he ignores all warnings that his life will be in danger and guilelessly and loyally accepts. In a visually interesting scene the Duke orders new cloaks for his guests and Archas is given the black robe of death. Boroskie now leads him off to torture, vowing to break his proud heart.

Archas's disbanded soldiers, meanwhile, have remained in the city disguised as broom-sellers and the like, singing such bouncy songs as "If your daughters on their beds, / Have bow'd, or crackt their maiden heads" (3.5.218) and providing rowdy comedy; at the news of his torture they revolt, commanded by Archas's son Theodore. The rescued Archas once more demonstrates his unfailing loyalty not only by putting down the rebellion but also by threatening to execute Theodore for treason.

He is only turned from this ultimate demonstration of loyalty by Putskie threatening to kill young Archas:

> behold young *Archas;*
> Behold thy brother here, thou bloody brother,
> As bloody to this sacrifice as thou art:
> Heave up thy sword, and mine's heav'd up: strike *Archas,*
> And I'le strike too, as suddenly, as deadly. . . .
> (5.6.257)

The Duke adds his royal command and the patriarch yields. The scene is highly pictorial and emblematic. The two sons are potentially sacrificial victims to the two brothers. The balanced opposites are posed in an heroic tableau at the precise moment of potential tragedy. "Have mercy, and I'le have mercy: the Duke gives it," says Putskie and the Duke commands, "On your obedience, / On your allegeance save him" (5.6.258), and Archas's loyalty now brings mercy. The balance now tilts to the comic, to repentance, forgiveness, and marriages. Archas has been willing to carry his loyalty to the ultimate, but to do so would outrage both reason and love.

Reason and love triumph when Archas obeys the Duke's command. We might argue therefore that reason and mercy do not in fact win, but that blind loyalty does. If we think of Fletcher as primarily concerned with themes, with making statements, such a conclusion seems unavoidable. But the play as a whole and the scene just described demonstrate once more that theme for Fletcher is always subservient to entertainment and emotion.

The chastity of Honora and Viola in the midst of the sexual corruption of the court parallels Archas's loyalty, his honorable father, and his chaste daughters, but it is difficult to agree with the view that "There can be no reasonable doubt that *The Loyal Subject* glorifies chastity."[13] When, after trying and failing to seduce Honora and Viola, the Duke declares, "Thou has done a cure upon me, counsell could not" (4.3.232), the point is not that the Duke "has passed a moral turning point in his life." Rather, it lies in the comic drama of his fickle reaction, when Alinda enters and he shatters his pose of virtue regained by returning the ring he gave her: "Why frownes my faire *Alinda?* / I have forgot both these againe" (4.3.232). The Duke has not reformed and Fletcher is not interested in showing the power of chastity. He is interested in a good scene that shows not the power of chastity but the persistence of lechery. When the Duke really reforms, he does so because it is a dramatic requirement of the fifth act of a Fletcherian tragicomedy. The moral and ethical issues of *The Loyal Subject* are the occasion for the dramatic entertainment and subordinate to that entertainment.

Anything Goes: Three Major Entertainments

The three plays to be considered here—*The Knight of Malta, The Humorous Lieutenant,* and *The Island Princess*—all reinforce the view of Fletcher as a playwright concerned first with entertainment, with strong scenes and roles, and only secondarily with thematic statements. All three plays have complex plots involving extreme and improbable situations in which characters have the opportunity of adopting various heroic, villainous, and comic stances expressed in language that is every bit as important as the stance. In all three, scene and language are paramount to theme and character.

The Knight of Malta (1616–19) is a collaborative work of Fletcher with, for the last time, Nathan Field, and for the first time Philip Massinger.[14] The collaboration explains inconsistencies and some of

the shifts in style, but *The Knight of Malta* is a good example of
piece-work playwriting by able professionals. Although the plot is
silly and the characters unreal, the play never lacks for moments of
excitement, and the actors are given numerous opportunities to
demonstrate their declamatory skills. The unreality of the characters
does not interfere with the theatrical potential they present to the
actors.

Zanthia, also known as Abdella, combines the wicked sexually
depraved female role with the added twist of being the Satanic black.
She encourages the fallen knight Montferrat in his depravity and
his threats against the chaste vision of purity, Oriana. Both Zanthia
and Montferrat are given ample opportunities to declare and demonstrate their villainies, and Montferrat is also allowed some moments of highly rhetorical declarations of guilt.

Virtuous characters are seldom if ever as interesting as villains,
but the actor playing the noble Miranda is allowed two major scenes
in which he tests Oriana's chastity by playing the seducer. Norandine, the bluff soldier role, has some good comic moments, including a drunk scene and an opportunity to startle the watch by
making pig noises (perhaps not a major chance for an actor but a
sure laugh) as well as proclaiming throughout the play the bouncy,
thick-skinned voice of reason in a world of high-flown rhetoric. The
setting, Malta, with its religious knights of various nationalities,
is appropriately exotic and romantic and allows for stage processions
and ceremonies and a quasi-religious atmosphere in which Mohammedanism and Christianity clash.

When Oriana rejects the advances of Montferrat, his mistress,
Oriana's servant, the wicked black woman Zanthia, who is known
as Abdella, forges a letter in Oriana's hand accepting the proposal
of the great Bashaw to convert to Mohammedanism and to marry
him. Her brother Valetta, the Grand Master of Malta, in the cheerfully sexist way brothers have in tragicomedy, immediately assumes
her guilty but allows her the right of trial by combat.

Of her suitors the Duke appoints Gomera her defender. Miranda,
however, is worried that Gomera is too old and weak to defeat the
accuser Montferrat. Therefore, he pretends to Montferrat that he
believes Oriana guilty and asks to take his place. Montferrat is a
recreant knight anyway and does not want to fight Gomera; so he
agrees. In the trial by combat, Miranda allows Gomera to defeat
him. When Gomera claims Oriana in marriage, Miranda reveals

himself and his reason for taking Montferrat's place and also claims Oriana. The Duke, however, awards her to Gomera because of his elder claim and because Miranda is destined to be married to the religious order of the Knights of Malta.

Oriana's troubles, of course, are not over. She marries Gomera and is soon pregnant, the occasion for some bawdy jests from Abdella, who sounds for the moment like Emilia in *Othello* or the Nurse in *Romeo and Juliet*. Oriana praises Miranda so enthusiastically (with more echoes of *Othello*) that Gomera becomes wildly jealous and accuses Oriana of infidelity. When Oriana faints, Abdella is on the spot to offer Gomera a curative potion for Oriana which puts her to sleep with the appearance of death. Abdella's plan is to win back Montferrat's favor by offering him the sleeping Oriana. Montferrat pleasantly assures Abdella that she can drown Oriana after he has satisfied his lust. Fortunately they arrive at the tomb too late. Oriana awakens and is rescued by Miranda. Gomera discovers Montferrat and challenges him to a duel. He wounds Montferrat, but Abdella shoots him. They are ready to start torturing Gomera when Norandine arrives with the watch and the villains are seized.

The real action of the play is over and the fifth act is filled with the news that Oriana has given birth to a son, a reprise of Miranda's testing of Oriana's chastity and loyalty to Gomera, the recognition scene when Gomera finds that Oriana is still alive, the ceremonial striping of Montferrat's knightly honor and the order that he marry Abdella, and finally Miranda's induction into the Knights of Malta.

The atmosphere of *The Knight of Malta* is romantic, heroic, and chivalric. Eugene M. Waith's summary remains pertinent: "Few Beaumont and Fletcher plays are so chivalric as *The Knight of Malta*, and not many carry the emotional exploitation of heroic values to such an extreme. Yet the subordination of character and theme to theatrical effect in this tragicomedy is typical of the plays as a group."[15] The intense theatricality of the play can easily be demonstrated by a look at act 2, which has been attributed to Fletcher alone.

The act opens with the entrance of Norandine, Miranda, and soldiers. A stage direction indicates "A Sea-fight within, alarm" (*W,* vol. 7; 2.1.94); the sound effects, of course, work of themselves to generate a degree of excitement. Norandine is wounded, but plays the bluff and comic hero, thanking Miranda for a timely rescue: "My *Turk* had *Turk'd* me else: but he has well paid for't. / Why

what a Sign for an Almanack h'as made me!" (2.1.95). When the
surgeon comes to dress his bleeding wounds, Norandine cheerfully
calls his blood "the sweat of honor" (2.1.96). His response to the
booty the soldiers now bring in is in the same bluffly comic heroic
tone:

> A goodly purchase; Is it for this we venture
> Our liberties and lives? what can all this do?
> Get me some dozen surfeits, some seven fresh whores,
> And twenty pot-Allies; and then I am virtuous:
> Lay the Knights part by, and that to pay the Soldier;
> This is mine own, I think I have deserv'd it:
> Come, now look to me, and grope me like a Chambermaid,
> I'll neither start nor squeak. . . .
>
> (2.1.97)

The language is typical of Fletcher's wit, stagily artificial while
seemingly natural. Norandine provides a comic contrast to the high
heroics of Miranda and his apparent realistic language in some measure validates the chivalric world. When the troops bring in the
prisoners, including the beautiful Luscinda, the language and the
scene become suddenly almost realistic:

> 1 Soldier.   Shall I have her Captain?
>
> 2 Soldier.   Or I?
>
> 3 Soldier.   I'll marry her.
>
> 4 Soldier.   Good Captain, I.
>
> 3 Soldier.   And make her a good *Christian;* lay hands off her;
>   I know she's mine.
>
> 2 Soldier.   I'll give my full share for her: have you no manners;
>   To thrust the woman so?
>
> Norandine.   Share her among ye;
>   And may she give ye as many hurts as I have,
>   And twice as many aches.
>
> (2.1.99)

Undoubtedly Fletcher's audience found the quarrel of soldiers over
a female more comic than we may, but the comedy is mixed with
realism and with terror that generates the shift of tone when Luscinda
begins her appeal to Norandine:

> I have lost my husband, Sir;
> You feel not that: him that I love; you care not:
> When fortune falls on you thus, you may grieve too:
> My liberty, I kneel not for; mine honor,
> (If ever virtuous honor toucht your heart yet)
> Make dear, and precious, Sir: you had a mother.
>   (2.1.99)

The rough soldier's noble heart is touched and Luscinda is delivered to the care of Miranda and eventual reunion with her husband. The strength of this scene is in its variety of appeal and in the ease with which the dramatic changes are rung.

The second scene is pure exposition. Miranda expresses his fear that Gomera will be defeated in the trial by combat and his fears are expressed in the language of chivalric romance:

> *Gomera's* old and stiff: and he may lose her,
> The winter of his years and wounds upon him:
> And yet he has done bravely hitherto;
> *Montferat's* fury in his heat of Summer,
> The whistling of his Sword like angry storms,
> Renting up life by th' roots, I have seen him scale
> As if a Falcon had run up a train,
> Clashing his warlike pinions, his steel'd Curasse,
> And at his pitch inmew the Town below him.
> I must do something.
>   (2.2.101)

The verse has a noble (and Shakespearean) ring and is a good moment for the actor. Further exposition brings in Collonna, a Christian who has escaped Turkish captivity by swimming ashore and who, it will turn out, is Luscinda's husband. Miranda takes him into his service and sends him to bring Luscinda from Norandine.

The third scene begins with a brief meeting of Montferrat and Abdella. She is given another opportunity to display her wickedness, her sexuality, and her aggressive masculinity:

> Have ye not still these arms, that Sword, that heart-whole?
> Is't not a man ye fight with, and an old man,
> A man half kill'd already? Am not I here?

> As lovely in my black to entertain thee,
> As high and full of heat to meet thy pleasures?
>
> (2.3.103)

Montferrat's weakness is revealed, preparing the audience for the
willingness with which he greets Miranda's proposal that he take
his place in the trial by combat. The Montferrat-Miranda scene is
more enjoyable for the audience because we know each one is playing
a role. Montferrat pretends reluctance to let Miranda take his place;
Miranda pretends he believes Oriana guilty.

Norandine is given a little more comedy with his physician as a
bridge to the trial by combat scene: *"Drums afar off. A low March."*
This clearly will be as spectacular as the stage allows, but the
spectacle includes an oratorical display for Oriana:

> Thus I ascend: nearer I hope to heaven,
> Nor doe I fear to tread this dark black Mansion:
> The Image of my grave, each foot we move,
> Goes to it still: each hour we leave behind us,
> Knols sadly toward it: My noble Brother
> For yet mine innocence dares call ye so,
> And you the friends to virtue, that come hither,
> The *Chorus* to this *Tragick Scaene*, behold me. . . .
>
> (2.5.110)

With a slight echo of Shakespeare, Oriana's plight is made noble,
dignified, and moving. The victory comes, Oriana is brought down
from the scaffold, the revelation that Miranda fought in Montferrat's
place is made; and Valetta chooses Gomera as husband for Oriana
and marriage to the Order of the Knights of Malta for Miranda.
There is drama in the surprising choice of the older man and in
Miranda's melancholy acceptance. But the act ends on an upbeat
note with the news that Montferrat has fled and Norandine's cheery
cry:

> Come, we'll have wenches man, and all brave things.
> —Let her go: we'll want no Mistresses,
> Good Swords, and good strong Armors.
>
> (2.5.115)

The act shows Fletcher's command of the stage and the range of theatrical possibilities he saw and used. The plot has been advanced expeditiously, but every opportunity to move the audience has been exploited.

The Humorous Lieutenant was written by Fletcher alone around 1619. Its plot is simpler and more direct than *The Knight of Malta,* perhaps because it is not collaborative. In one of the few, if not the only reference to Fletcher in modern fiction, in Anthony Powell's *Hearing Secret Harmonies,* Delavacquerie takes Russell Gwinnet to a production of *A Humorous Lieutenant* and explains the comic plot in which the Lieutenant "was suffering from a go of the pox. Having a dose made him unusually brave. . . ."[16] The humors of the Lieutenant alternate with the tragicomic materials of the trials and loves of Demetrius and Evanthe whose names provided the title for a manuscript of the play prepared in 1625 by the scribe Ralph Crane for Sir Kenelm Digby, "the most accomplished Cavalier of his time," who also in 1625 secretly married the beautiful and notorious Venetia Stanley, sometime mistress of the earl of Dorset, "much against the good will of his mother, but he would say that a wise man, and a lusty, could make an honest woman out of a Brothell-house."[17]

The Humorous Lieutenant is a lively and entertaining play. Its popularity after the Restoration, and presumably before, rested on its comic vitality, sensationalism, and characters who, although belonging clearly enough to the theatrical stock of the day and meeting the type-casting demands of the repertory company, are touched with original life. Beyond sheer entertainment—drums, bugles, heroics, rhetoric, pathos, farce, satire, and wit—the play suggests another level of enjoyment in its double use of the abstract values of tragicomedy, both mocking and accepting. Chivalry is at one moment genuine coin and in the next a worthless counterfeit. Sex, expressed in the rhetoric of chastity, is a solemn matter, at the deep core of character and civilization; the scene shifts and the language, and sex is the heart of the human comedy. *The Humorous Lieutenant* for all its absurd plot, albeit no more absurd than many or any other Fletcherian tragicomedies, is marked by a distinct urbanity of tone.

The opening scene is a brilliant bit of realistic stage comedy as two ushers and attendant grooms with perfumes prepare the court presence chamber for the King's audience with the ambassadors of

the enemy kings. The language is sprightly and edged as they direct
ladies and gentlemen to their places:

> Make all things perfect: would you have these Ladies,
> They that come here to see the Show, these Beuties
> That have been labouring to set-off their Sweetnes,
> And washd, and curld; perfum'd, and taken Glisters,
> For feare a flaw of wind might over-take 'em,
> Lose these, and all their expectations?
> Madams, the best way is the upper-lodgings,
> There you may see at ease.
>
> $\qquad\qquad\qquad\qquad$ (*DW*, vol. 5; 1.1.305)

Citizens and their wives are shooed off with aristocratic disdain and
then enter "Celia *in poore attire.*" The audience will learn her identity
at the end of the play, but her opening lines hint that she is not
what she seems:

> I wou'd faine see him:
> The glory of this place, makes me remember,
> But dye those thoughts, dye all but my desires,
> Even those to death are sicke too; he's not here,
> Nor how my eyes may guide me—
>
> $\qquad\qquad\qquad\qquad$ (1.1.306)

Celia easily defeats the rudeness of the first usher and wins the
sympathy and sexual interest of the second. The entrance of King
Antigonus and the ambassadors introduces the political-military
theme. Prince Demetrius is given his own heroic entrance with
suitable attention to love and war. To Celia's intense admiration—
"Now a god speaks: / O I could dwell upon that tongue forever"
(1.1.312)—he hurls defiance at the ambassadors and declares for
war. He begs and wins from his father command of the troops and
the opportunity to gain his own military fame and honor.

Demetrius's attentive conversation with Celia produces a remarkable change in the ushers who now become all subservience
and service; it is also observed by King Antigonus who inquires
closely after her identity. With the introduction of the Lieutenant
and his peculiar humor and a romantic scene between Celia and
Demetrius the main plot lines are established. It is not until later,
however, that we come to realize that the King's interest in Celia

is predatory. The King's attempts to bed Celia, his son's love, provide the sexual twist to the play, the perverse note that gives piquancy to the otherwise bland and familiar plot of the captive princess who loves her captor.

The turn given to Demetrius's introduction to combat is that he begins with defeat and his desire to make a risky counterattack is mocked by the experienced Leontius, his military mentor, and by the Lieutenant. Demetrius frets about his lost honor, but Leontius and the Lieutenant are practical soldiers. The Lieutenant is especially biting about battlefield heroics. A host of young men have been lost in a pointless charge:

> They'l never ride o're other mens corne again, I take it,
> Such frisking, and such flaunting with their feathers,
> And such careering with their mistres favours:
> And here must he be pricking out for honor,
> And there got he a knocke, and down goes pilgarlike,
> Commends his soule to his she-saint, and *exit.*
> Another spurres in there, cryes make roome villaines,
> I am a Lord, scarce spoken, but with reverence,
> A rascall takes him o're the face, and fels him;
> There lyes the Lord, the Lord be with him.
>
> (2.2.327)

The stance is unequivocally realistic and antichivalric. Fletcher, of course, can and does easily slip into the heroic and the chivalric tragicomic mode, but in a sense the damage has been done. The heroic rhetoric of the play has been qualified; the sounding trumpets will hint of tin.

So it is with the aging and raging lust of the King. For all his hot pursuit of his son's beloved, not merely a case of May and December but spiritually, if not technically, incestuous, Antigonus remains basically comic. The scale of his lust, we are given to understand, is gargantuan. It is maintained by a bureaucracy of bawds run by a fat administratrix named Leucippe who keeps elaborate books on the girls available for the appetites of King and court:

> She is not fifteen they say: for her complexion—
> *Cloe, Cloe, Cloe,* here, I have her,
> *Cloe, the Daughter of a Countrey gentleman;*
> *Her age upon fifteen:* now her *complexion,*

A *lovely browne;* here 'tis; *eyes black and rolling,*
The body neatly built: she strikes a Lute well,
Sings most inticingly: these helps consider'd,
Her maiden-head will amount to some three hundred,
Or three hundred and fifty crowns; 'twil bear it handsomly.
Her father's poore, some little share deducted,
To buy him a hunting Nag; I 'twill be pretty:
Who takes care of the Merchants wife?

> (2.3.329)

Leucippe is hardly attractive, but she is one of those characters whose wickedness cannot be taken very seriously; she is a comic grotesque rather than anything really evil. There is a minor joke in the fact that the names of the girls in her files are all drawn from romance literature—Cloe, Thisbe, Phebe, Altea, and the like.

Nor is the King's pursuit of Cloe ever deeply threatening to her; she not only retains her equilibrium, but her wit and sharp tongue give her a decided advantage over Antigonus. When his attempts at seduction fail, he resorts to a magician to produce a charmed aphrodisiacal potion. The conjuring scene provides opportunity for song and spectacle: *"Sweete Musique is heard, and an Antick of litle* Fayeries *enter, and dance about the Bowle, and fling in things"* (4.3.377). When Samuel Pepys saw *The Humorous Lieutenant* in 1667, he found it "a silly play" but admired the special effects that had been added to the conjuring scene: "the Spirit in it that grows very tall, and then sinks again to nothing, having two heads breeding upon one."[18] It is unlikely that Fletcher would have objected to any liberties that would expand its theatricality.

"God-a-mercie deare December," Cloe remarks aside and then proceeds to savage the King with lines that recall Hamlet's to Polonius:

I am reading sir of a short Treatise here,
Thats call'd the vanity of lust: has your Grace seene it?
He sayes here, that an old mans loose desire
Is like a glow-wormes light, the Apes so wonder'd at:
Which when they gather'd sticks, and laid upon't,
And blew, and blew, turn'd taile, and went out presently:
And in another place, he cals their loves,
Faint smels of dying flowers. . . .

> (4.5.387)

The King's machinations come to naught when the Lieutenant swallows the potion and falls in love with Antigonus. "He lookes," says the King of the doting soldier, "as if he were bepist . . ." (5.1.400). Demetrius is allowed a scene of ranting jealousy. He has little reason to distrust Celia, and his temper tantrum is simply a way of introducing a dramatic delay before the resolution with a bit of rhetorical fireworks.

The Humorous Lieutenant's world is essentially comic. Its tragicomic intensities are qualified by a mocking double vision. The corruption of King and court is without any real darkness. The heroics of the young prince and his chivalrous opponents are qualified by the realism and antichivalric attitudes of Leontius and the Lieutenant. Celia herself is essentially a comic heroine—witty, self-reliant, and well able to handle the bumbling sexual corruption of Antigonus's court. If the joke of the humor of the Lieutenant is a bit thin, The Humorous Lieutenant is a thoroughly lively and entertaining play that shows Fletcher at close to his comic best.

The Island Princess was written about 1620–21 and is also attributed solely to Fletcher. The story is derived from a French novel, L'histoire de Ruis Dias et de Quixaire, princesse des Moloques (1615), by Le Sr de Bellan. The novel was in turn based on Bartolomé Leonardo de Argensola's Conquista de las Islas Malucas (1609). The play is set in the exotic Moluccas, the Spice Islands, in the Malay Archipelago. In revised forms it was popular in the Restoration and in 1699 was performed as an opera. The spectacular potential of the play is clear in Samuel Pepys's notation that "it is a pretty good play, many good things being in it, and a good scene of a town on fire."[19]

The "good things" in The Island Princess are its patina of romance, heroics both military and religious, and a neat and uncluttered plot. The setting and the plot might have been worked to reflect on the conflict of East and West and of Christian and pagan, but Fletcher is not interested in these themes except for their rhetorical and theatrical possibilities. Armusia, the Portuguese hero, is willing, almost anxious, to die for his faith; and his faith wins Princess Quisara to Christianity and at least begins the conversion of the King. Quisara, however, is an impressionable young lady whose attitudes are controlled by dramatic rather than thematic needs.

Armusia's "We are arriv'd among the blessed Islands, / Where every wind that rises blowes perfumes" (DW, vol. 5; 1.3.561) is

an attempt to evoke the setting, but the islands are always hazy and
finally any foreign place might do as well. Except for the King of
Tidore, the brother of the Princess, who is immensely heroic and
long suffering at the start of the play, the natives are a doubtful
lot, stereotypically deserving of colonization. The two kings who
court Quisara, including the King of Bakam, a "fellow that farts
terrour" (1.3.562), are ineffectual and mildly comic. The Governor
of the island of Ternata is a thoroughly bad lot, a stock stage villain.

The King of Tidore has been captured by the Governor of Ternata.
The Princess informs her suitors—two native kings, the Portuguese
captain Ruy Dias, and the King's captor, the Governor of Ternata—
that she will marry the man who rescues her brother from captivity.
She scornfully rejects the Governor's offer to release the King in
return for her hand and the Governor furiously vows to make her
brother's imprisonment as nasty as possible.

Quisara's rudeness to the Governor would be grotesquely irrational
in any world but that of tragicomedy; here its rationale is as dramatic
as her risky romantic challenge. She expects the dashing Ruy Dias
to seize the moment but he reacts reasonably rather than romantically
and chivalrously:

> Your Grace must give me leave to looke about me,
> And take a little time, the cause will aske it,
> Great acts require great counsells.
>
>   (1.3.566)

The newly arrived Armusia is not so cautious. He immediately
conceives a plan of rescue and sets about it. Ruy Dias's caution is
sharply contrasted with Armusia's immediate heroic activity.

Act 2 shows in quick succession the sufferings of the King and
his rescue: "King appeares loaden with chaines; his head, arms only
above [the stage trapdoor]" (2.1.570). The Governor arrives to taunt
him and the King's noble pathos is set against the Governor's malignant cruelty. The emotional scene is followed by bells ringing,
explosions, smoke and fire, and a moment of citizen comedy—
"Body o me neighbours there's fire in my codpiece" (2.4.581)—
with Armusia's rescue of the King.

Quisara, meanwhile, has been chiding Ruy Dias for his inactivity.
Just as he resolves to act there is a great shout and Armusia trium-
phantly returns with the King. Ruy Dias's shame and anguish

deepen when Armusia claims the prize, Quisara. Quisara shows her deep reluctance; Ruy Dias was to have been her brother's savior, not this stranger. The plot now takes a turn and focuses on the failed hero, Ruy Dias, who launches a counterplot, asking his nephew Pyniero to help kill Armusia. Pyniero pretends sympathy while punctuating the conversation with satiric asides:

> What malicious soule does this man carry?
> And to what scurvy things this love converts us?
> What stinking things, and how sweetly they become us?
> Murther's a morall vertue with these Lovers,
> A special peece of Divinitie I take it. . . .
>
> (3.1.592)

Pyniero adds a further twist to the action by not only getting Quisara to agree to the murder of Armusia but also by wooing her in his own right and turning her from Ruy Dias.

If consistency of characterization were a matter of concern in *The Island Princess,* we would agree with Pyniero's description of Quisara, "This woman's cunning, but she's bloudy too; / Although she pulls her Tallons in, she's mischievous" (3.1.598). But we are not to draw conclusions about Quisara; her shifts are the consequence of plot and the need for theatrics. Her character is measured in scenes.

Her point of view changes drastically again when Armusia bribes Quisara's servant and gains entrance to her bedroom. Armusia persuades her that he has not come to rape her, declares his love, and wins her admiration when, expressing perfect confidence in her chastity, he leaves her alone with Ruy Dias. Quisara's aside—"What a pure soule inherits here? What innocence?" (3.3.607)—signals another shift in her affections.

In no time at all Quisara has been transformed from potential villainess in a tale of murderous love back into a romantic heroine. Ruy Dias also begins a character transformation when he abandons his plan to have Armusia murdered and challenges him to a duel instead. Armusia defeats Ruy Dias, but at Quisara's request lets him live and, moreover, makes honorable peace with him. Ruy Dias has recovered his lost honor and declares "Now to be honorable even with this Gentleman, / Shall be my businesse, and my ends his" (4.3.621).

Quisara agrees to marry Armusia if he will abandon Christianity.

His response is instantaneous: "I'le be hang'd first" (4.5.623). Not content with this simple denial, he expands at length on his contempt for Quisara's false religion and for the poor girl herself:

> I hate and curse ye,
> Contemne your deities, spurne their powers,
> And where I meet your maumet Gods, I'le swing 'em
> Thus o're my head, and kick 'em into puddles,
> Nay I will out of vengeance search your Temples,
> And with those hearts that serve my God, demolish
> Your shambles of wild worships.
>
> (4.5.625)

The Governor, now disguised as "a Moorish priest," has been turning the King against the Portuguese and seizes this opportunity to have Armusia imprisoned for his blasphemy, calling for fires and tortures to make him abandon his faith. The next turn in the plot is Quisara's conversion to Christianity, so impressed is she by Armusia's defiance and faith:

> Your faith, and your religion must be like ye,
> They that can shew you these, must be pure mirrours;
> When the streames flow cleare and pure, what are the fountaines.
>
> (5.2.633)

This conversion is another moment for heightened language and emotion; it is not of thematic importance. Ruy Dias meanwhile has seized the fortress and with his Portuguese won the day. The Governor's false beard and hair are plucked off and he is sent to prison to repent. The King is half converted. Armusia and Quisara will wed, and Ruy Dias's honor is fully restored.

From this summary it should appear that *The Island Princess* is a busy play, crowded with spectacle, romance, heroics, a touch of religion, and plenty of surface emotion. Ruy Dias regains his heroic virtue, but he only lost it for reasons of the plot. Quisara's own changes—initial love for Ruy Dias, rejection of Armusia, strong interest in Pyniero, love for Armusia—are also explained by the requirements of the plot. We are not to conclude she is worthlessly flighty because we are not expected to think of her as a character except in relation to the theatrical needs of individual scenes. *The*

Island Princess asks of its audience only a willingness to be entertained and in return it offers varied and lively entertainment.

The Perfected Style: *A Wife for a Month*

A Wife for a Month was licensed in May of 1624 and is one of Fletcher's last plays and the last tragicomedy he wrote alone. It can be seen as a summation of his tragicomic practice. It shows the playwright in complete control of the dramatic potentials of his materials and his actors. *A Wife for a Month* is marked by its sheer professionalism, but also by an intrusive comic spirit that at times mocks the tragicomic form in which it is found. The themes of honor and chastity provide the grist for the dramatic mill, but Fletcher's concerns in the play are theatrical rather than thematic. Although objection has been made to the play's somewhat perverse sexuality and lewdness, its theatricality has been unchallenged.

The improbable hypothesis of *A Wife for a Month* bears some relation to *The Mad Lover* in that a poetic hyperbole is taken literally and the main action is based on the working out of that conceit. Frederick, the usurping King of Naples, is one of Fletcher's many lecherous monarchs. His lechery is assisted by Sorano, the brother of Evanthe, the lady who is the object of the royal lechery. The chaste and virtuous Evanthe is in love with Valerio and strenuously rejects the King's advances. When the King obtains a love poem in which Valerio vows to Evanthe that "To be your own but one poor Month, I'd give / My Youth, my Fortune, and then leave to live" (*W*, vol. 5; 1.1.11), the King designs his outrageous revenge on this lover's hyperbole. He will grant Valerio his wish to marry Evanthe, but at the end of a month he will be executed and Evanthe will have to take another husband or die. In the nineteenth century W. S. Gilbert made high comic use of the theme of the wife for a month in *The Mikado*.

The relative Gilbertian innocence of the King's revenge, however, is not sufficient for Sorano, who gives it a far nastier and perverse twist. If Valerio consummates the marriage, Evanthe will be killed. If he reveals the reason for his behavior—or lack of it—they both will be killed. We are not to worry how the King and Sorano would know either if the marriage had been consummated or what Valerio would tell or not tell Evanthe. We are to enjoy the extremity of this variation on the story of Tantalus.

The subplot provides the solution to the dilemma. As well as
scheming against his sister and Valerio, Sorano has promised Frederick that he will kill Frederick's brother, Alphonso, the true king
who has retired to a monastery to mourn his father's death and nurse
a mysterious melancholic disease. Sorano convinces Alphonso's
guardians that he has a cure for Alphonso's illness and demonstrates
the potion's safety by swallowing it himself. It is, of course, a poison
for which the crafty Sorano has taken an antidote. The plot misfires
because of the peculiar pathology of Alphonso's disease. The poison's
heat counteracts the disabling cold of the malady and Alphonso is
cured. He regains his throne and sends the wretched Frederick and
the nasty Sorano to a monastery to study repentance. Evanthe and
Valerio are free to consummate their marriage.

With such a tale a basic problem is to keep the action moving
and to sustain its sensationalism through variations of tone and the
manipulation of dramatic peaks. The wickedness of the King and
Sorano is mixed with comedy; both are villains, but both are also
partly comic. The opening dialogue is carefully modulated to create
a variety of effects. The King cautiously tiptoes to his declaration
that he lusts after Sorano's sister and wants Sorano to pimp for him,
but the delicacy is wasted on Sorano. The King can have his sister:

> And if I had a dozen more, they were all yours:
> Some Aunts I have, they have been handsome Women,
> My Mother's dead indeed, and some few Cousins
> That are now shooting up, we shall see shortly.
>   (1.1.3)

The language transforms the villain into a comic gargoyle. "My
Mother's dead indeed" may be not especially tasteful, but it is
superbly outrageous. Fletcher's command of comic language is sure
and deft. The laughter clears the way for the next emotional peak,
but it also influences our response to those peaks.

When Frederick propositions Evanthe, the tone shifts from gar-
goylish comic bawdry to the heroics of female honor, chastity:

> I had rather be a Whore, and with less sin,
> To your present lust, than Queen to your injustice.
> Yours is no love, Faith and Religion fly it,
> Nor has no taste of fair affection in it. . . .
>   (1.1.6)

Evanthe's language is imaginative and vigorous; her figures are striking:

> I would first take to me, for my lust, a Moor,
> One of your Gally-slaves, that cold and hunger,
> Decrepit misery, had made a mock-man,
> Than be your Queen.
>
> (1.1.7)

There is an added irony that Valerio will be forced to present himself to Evanthe as "mock-man." The boy playing Evanthe is given plenty of room for histrionics:

> I had rather be a Leper, and be shun'd,
> And dye by pieces, rot into my grave,
> Leaving no memory behind to know me,
> Than be a high Whore to eternity.
>
> (1.1.7)

Such language does not call for subtlety but for an ability to reach for extremes, to play the passions for all they are worth.

When the Queen sees the King and Sorano scuttle away at her entrance, she suspects the worst of Evanthe, who rather cruelly allows the Queen to think that she is indeed willing to replace her. Only when the Queen weeps does Evanthe express her sympathy and her firm resolve to chastity. The scene is a small example of Fletcher's skill at scene building by the use of the unexpected and by tonal shifts. Evanthe's behavior is explicable not by her character but by the need to build to an emotional peak that will not simply repeat her previous rhetoric of chastity.

Perhaps Fletcher's strongest hand is in the fast pace of the variety of his scenes. Evanthe furiously scolds her maid Cassandra, in the role of the comic old bawd, for having let Sorano get the casket in which Valerio's love poem was found. The King sarcastically breaks in upon her, scolding: "Has your young sanctity done railing, madam?" Cassandra in her turn chastises Sorano's servant Podrano until the King silences her:

> Peace good Antiquity, I'll have your Bones else
> Ground into Gunpowder to shoot Cats with;

One word more, and I'll blanch thee like an almond,
There's no such cure for the she-falling sickness
As powder of a dryed Bawd Skin, be silent.
                                        (1.1.13–14)

With the audience roaring with laughter at this billingsgate, Fletcher deftly switches the tone. Frederick pronounces his sentence on Valerio and Evanthe. Then the couple are left alone on the stage to savor briefly the bitter sweetness of a month of marriage with death at its end. In a short space Fletcher has deftly moved us from rollicking laughter to quiet pathos.

Of course their bittersweet expectations will turn sour with the nasty twist Sorano and Frederick give to the marriage, "the exquisite vexation," as Sorano has it. The potential of the marriage night is masterfully exploited. Evanthe, already established as tough-minded and independent, is not a blushing and retiring bride, but eager and forward. There is not a jot of sexual repression in her. Valerio must play the reluctant bridegroom. He attempts a Neoplatonic argument, but Evanthe will have none of it. As a last resort he declares he is impotent, and Evanthe with sweet and loving resignation accepts the unhappy state of things: "All fond desire dye here, and welcome chastity, Honour and chastity . . ." (3.1.39). The audience knows that Valerio is lying because he has been forbidden to reveal the real reason for not consummating the marriage—the threat of Evanthe's death. Sorano has been coarsely explicit:

                    if you hit her,
        Be sure you hit her home, and kill her with it;
        There are such women that will dye with pleasure:
        The Axe will follow else, that will not fail
        To fetch her Maiden head, and dispatch her quickly.
                                        (3.1.30)

The scene is complex and multilayered.

In the abstract A Wife for a Month suggests a strange psychological fairy tale. Death is the consequence of sexuality until the malign charm is broken by the restoration of the usurped king, a restoration effected by a poison that turns out not to be poison but medicine, the medicine like passion producing creative heat. But the real force of the play is in its theatricality, its varied language, and its mix of comic and quasi-tragic tones.

If there is pathos in frustrated passion, there is also comedy. Impotence may be solemn enough in real life and business for sexologists, but on the stage it is always potentially comic. Valerio's claim of impotence cannot escape the comic; and the basic situation, the lovers perched on the brink of the bed and prevented, reaches back to the Old Comedy of the Greeks. Valerio's teenaged hyperbole, the conceit on which the play turns, is comic in the largest sense of the word; or perhaps it is the very quintessence of tragicomedy.

This discussion has been limited to Fletcher's major tragicomedies, but the plays we have not discussed follow similar patterns. Characterization is strongly influenced by the actors of the repertory company. The scene is of greatest importance and both character and theme will be cheerfully sacrificed to the dramatic moment. The improbable situation, the concern with rhetorical language and acting style, the stylization of the witty conceit, and the pervasive awareness of the comic all contribute to the unabashed self-conscious theatricality of the tragicomedies. At their best these plays are the work of a master craftsman thoroughly at home in the theater, who writes with sure control of the possibilities to be found in his stage, actors, and the dramatic materials of his day.

Chapter Four

"No Buskin Shew'd More Solemne": The Tragedies

John Fletcher wrote eight tragedies, six of them in collaboration and two by himself. The tragedies are often interesting, lively, and theatrically valid; but the form does not represent a major interest or strength on Fletcher's part. His art is not really attuned to the tragic. The major difference between the tragedies and the tragicomedies is that the tragedies have deaths, not that they evoke or express a tragic consciousness.

In *Thierry and Theodoret,* for example, Theodoret is murdered and then his brother is killed with a poisoned handkerchief; their nasty mother, the cause of their deaths, is finally executed. The world of *Thierry and Theodoret* is violent, lurid, and unnatural, but it is not tragic in the larger sense of the word. Its events seem too extraordinary, beyond the normal run of things. The link between character and action is either tenuous or too obvious and the play offers no larger vision of life. There is a bit too much blood to turn *Thierry and Theodoret* easily into a tragicomedy, but its darkness is not much different from the dark passages of the tragicomedies and the task would not be insurmountable.

The abstract and simplified characters of tragicomedy, the chaste heroine, the honorable soldier, the loyal hero, the evil woman, characters who embody ideals and their opposites, are translated to the fatal settings of tragedy. This bare, single-focused characterization has led one critic to argue that Fletcher "is already strongly tainted with the spirit of classicism, or rather neo-classicism, and that is perhaps the most characteristic feature of his development."[1] Such a view reaffirms Fletcher's position as a transitional figure pointing the way to the heroic drama of the Restoration. The concentration on character types rather than on individual characteristics results in greater emphasis on rhetorical display and on the emotional and spectacular qualities of individual scenes.

In the essay just cited Marco Mincoff strenuously objects that to see Fletcher as "an excellent purveyor of commercial drama for the gentry is to condemn him more uncompromisingly than his worst detractors to the ranks of the third rate." This assertion underlines a fairly consistent unwillingness in critical commentary on Fletcher to accept and recognize his real merit—his skill as a professional playwright. His powers as an entertainer are seen as rather shameful, and he must be rescued and made important through his incipient neoclassicism, his royalist or antiroyalist political concerns, or his representation of shifting social currents and thoughts.

But John Fletcher was a professional playwright, earning his living by supplying the voracious appetite of the London stage with plays. The strengths of his tragedies are in their stagecraft, in technical control of the medium, in their ability to entertain the audience of his own day and that of half a century beyond. Playwrights, film writers, and television writers who work collectively do so most frequently for economic reasons—because collaboration is an effective way to meet deadlines and to increase production, not because it is the best way to express an individual artistic vision. That so much of Fletcher's work is collaborative reflects his professionalism. His tragedies can be read without embarrassment or apology as the commercial drama they are, entertainments that earned him his living, judging by his position, reputation, and even by his portrait, a handsome one.

With the exception of *The Maid's Tragedy* and its stunning frustrated-wedding-night scene, the tragedies are as difficult to recall in detail as the tragicomedies. Plots are complex and detailed; characters are generalized types. The language is clear and easily understood, the quality so admired in the later seventeenth century, but not memorable. These negative features, however, do not define Fletcher's achievements in tragedy. Clifford Leech, admitting the unmemorability of the tragedies, puts the case with accuracy and generosity: "It is always a pleasure to reread Fletcher, not because each reading has more to reveal, but because we have forgotten how shrewd and intricate the writing and its insights are."[2] To which it is essential to add how dramatically skilled the writing is.

The Maid's Tragedy

The Maid's Tragedy was written by Beaumont and Fletcher between 1608 and 1611 and with *Philaster* and *A King and No King* represents the peak of their collaborative success. On the basis of linguistic evidence four scenes have been attributed to Fletcher: 2.2, 2, 4.1, and 5.1–2.[3] However, we need to remind ourselves again that the details of the collaboration are not really known. The interchange of ideas, the talking back and forth before a scene is actually written, make certainty of attribution impossible. The real point concerning the collaborative effort of *The Maid's Tragedy* is that, linguistic determiners aside, the work is so seamless and polished. Those scenes attributed to Fletcher, moreover, are of central importance to the play.

No direct source is known for the plot; but the complicated situations and the romantic atmosphere, the dialectical play with various themes of honor and love recall both Sidney's *Arcadia* and the lengthy French romance of Honoré d'Urfé, *L'Astreé*. The relationship of *The Maid's Tragedy* to *Hamlet* is pervasive and provocative. H. Neville Davis ends an essay on the subject by wryly commenting, "Oh, that it should come to this, and Shakespeare's play scarce ten years on the boards."[4] His discomfiture may have been increased by seeing both *The Maid's Tragedy* and *Hamlet* played in repertory at Stratford-on-Avon by the Royal Shakespeare Company in 1980.

The comparison of any play in the Fletcher canon with Shakespeare, however, is likely to produce a wry, if not pained, remark, and *The Maid's Tragedy* has called forth pained remarks quite on its own, without reference to Shakespeare. In 1678, when neoclassicism was beginning to work against the popularity of Beaumont and Fletcher, Thomas Rhymer complained in *The Tragedies of the Last Age* that "nothing in *History* was ever so *unnatural,* nothing in *Nature* was ever so *improbable,* as we find the whole conduct of this Tragedy,—so far are we from any thing accurate and Philosophical as Poetry requires."[5] Subsequent objections to the play, as to Fletcher's "serious" plays in general, focus on improbability and lack of real seriousness, but their theatricality is unchallenged, even when it is denigrated.

The plot of *The Maid's Tragedy* is indeed sensational. Amintor, who planned to marry Aspatia, obeys the King's command to marry Evadne. On their wedding night he learns that Evadne is the King's mistress and that he has become the King's convenient cuckold to mask the affair. Shamed and disgraced as he is, Amintor is unable to revenge himself upon the King because of his profound monarchal loyalty. It remains for Evadne's brother, Amintor's friend Melantius, to bring about the death of the King and the revenge of Amintor as well as of his own and his sister's family honor. He convinces Evadne to kill the King. Aspatia in her grief disguises herself as a man and, claiming to be her own brother, taunts Amintor to a fight in which he fatally stabs her. Evadne commits suicide and Amintor follows suit. The new King proclaims the moral:

> May this a faire example be to me,
> To rule with temper, for on lustfull Kings
> Unlookt for suddaine deaths from God are sent,
> But curst is he that is their instrument.
> (DW, vol. 2; 5.3.124)

This resolves the question of the propriety of assassinating wicked kings, but emphasizes the unfocused quality of the play's ending. It is not on Aspatia, who is the tragic maiden, nor on Amintor, whose betrayal of Aspatia, a betrayal resulting from his conception of duty and his misreading of honor as public reputation, is an essential ingredient to the tragedy.

The Maid's Tragedy was included in a list of plays presented during the celebration of the marriage of King James's daughter Elizabeth to Count Frederick, the Elector Palatine of the Rhine, in 1613. It may strike us as a rather tasteless choice for a wedding celebration, but points to the play's dramatic success and suggests that its approach to kingship gave no offense.

In a letter to his friend the diplomat Dudley Carleton, John Chamberlain reports at length on the extravagant wedding celebration of the princess and Count Frederick and reports that "The next morning the King went to visit these young turtles that were coupled on St. Valentine's day, and did strictly examine him whether he were his true son-in-law, and was sufficiently assured."[6] Such a visit would be a less bizarre procedure for a dynastic wedding in the seventeenth century than it seems to us, but it can serve as a reminder of the extent to which *The Maid's Tragedy* and other Fletcherian plays mirror their times with varying degrees of precision and distortion. The King's close questioning of Amintor after the wedding night is dramatically apropos, but it would also not be an unfamiliar reflection of current customs.

The major and most popular scenes derive much of their interest from such varied and shifting reflections as well as from their studied

theatricality. The play opens with courtiers chatting of the prepa-
rations for the wedding masque and supplying a direct and accurate
prescription for such performances:

> they must commend their King, and speake in praise
> Of the assembly, blesse the Bride and Bridegroome,
> In person of some god, there tied to rules
> Of flatterie.

(1.1.29)

Thus the masque, the epitome of courtly pretense and artifice, is
unmasked and the audience prepared to watch the coming show
with an alert cynicism. The masque itself fits the description well
enough. Moreover, it recalls *The Murder of Gonzago,* the play-within-
a-play in *Hamlet,* in the complexity of responses it will evoke from
its two audiences, those within the play and those outside, the real
audience of *The Maid's Tragedy.*

The abandoned and aggrieved Aspatia will suggest Ophelia. Her
father, Calianax, plays the *senex,* the old man, Polonius's part. The
masque will be watched with a difference by those of the court aware
of the King's order that Amintor break his betrothal to Aspatia to
marry Evadne. Evadne and the King, conspiring lovers, will watch
still differently. *"Stay, Stay, and hide / the blushes of the Bride"* (1.2.43)
and all the epithalamional trappings of the masque will seem pos-
itively sinister upon reflection, after the revelation of Evadne's relationship with the King; the possibilities for varied and suggestive
reactions to the masque by the courtiers are manifest.

At the very least, the formal, ritualized masque makes an effective
contrast with the brilliant drama of Evadne's revelation to Amintor
that she is the King's mistress. Evadne's surprise is further set up
by Aspatia's Ophelia-like lament, *"Lay a garland on my hearse,"* to
which Evadne outrageously responds by having one of her maids
sing a libertine and indeed cavalier *"I could never have the power / To
love one above an houre"* (2.1.49). The forlorn Aspatia bestows a last
fond kiss on Amintor, leaving him to admit and quickly rationalize
his betrayal in soliloquy:

> my guilt is not so great
> As mine owne conscience, too sencible,
> Would make me thinke, I onely breake a promise,

> And twas the King that forst me: timerous flesh,
> Why shakst thou so?
>
> (2.1.51)

Evadne's entrance immediately erases any remaining scruples, and Amintor's desire is made clear as he urges Evadne to bed only to be met with her astounding refusal. To Amintor's suggestion that she has innocently vowed to a girl friend to keep her virginity for one night, she scornfully replies in undoubtedly the most famous line of the play: "A maidenhead *Amintor* / At my years?" (2.1.53).

The shocking revelations in the scene are carefully parcelled out: first Evadne's refusal and finally this climax:

Evadne.	Why tis the King.
Amintor.	The King.
Evadne.	What will you do now?
Amintor.	Tis not the King.
Evadne.	What did he make this match for dull *Amintor?*
Amintor.	Oh thou hast nam'd a word that wipes away
	All thoughts revengefull, in that sacred name,
	The King, there lies a terror, what fraile man
	Dares lift his hand against it? let the Gods
	Speake to him when they please, till when let us
	Suffer, and waite.

> (2.1.57)

We have been prepared for Amintor's extreme royalism; he abandoned Aspatia at the King's command, but his compliance here is still shocking. Moreover, it defeats the audience's expectations for rage and a vow of revenge. The development of the revenge plot must wait; and the avenger will be Melantius, not Amintor. At one level Amintor's response is a dramatic device to increase suspense and complexity of plot. The complexity and psychological, even sociological, sophistication of the scene is further increased by the next step in Amintor's reaction:

> me thinkes I am not wrong'd,
> Nor is it ought, if from the censuring world
> I can but hide it—reputation
> Thou art a word, no more,—but thou hast showne

An impudence so high, that to the world
I feare thou wilt betray or shame thy selfe.

                                         (2.1.58)

Amintor perverts the great Renaissance value of honor to mere
reputation and by doing so not only accepts the corruption of the
King and Evadne, but actively participates in it, accepting the loss
of his honor to preserve his reputation.

The scene ends with Evadne and Amintor strangely joined, married in the lie that they will play the married couple:

                     now I resolve
He has dishonour'd thee: give me thy hand,
Be careful of thy credit, and sinne close,
Tis all I wish; upon thy chamber floure
Ile rest to night, that morning visitors
May thinke we did as married people use. . . .

                                         (2.1.59)

The wit of the scene extends beyond shock, surprise, or the sublim-
inal comedy of sexual frustration to the complex distortions of the
fun-house mirror.

In the bawdy badinage with which the courtiers greet the supposed happy couple Amintor so overacts that Evadne must toss him
a whispered aside, "You do it scurvily, twill be perceiv'd" (3.1.67).
But not, it happens, so scurvily that the King himself is not deceived
and his jealousy aroused.

King.	Tell me then, how shewes the sport
	Unto thee?
Amintor.	Why well?
King.	What did you doe?
Amintor.	No more nor lesse then other couples use,
	You know what tis, it has but a course name.

                                         (3.1.68)

The King's salacious questions are, of course, outrageous taunts,
the harem master teasing his eunuch, but Amintor plays his role
with such skill that his responses coupled with Evadne's own am-
biguous answers push the King to an accusation:

> I see there is no lasting faith in sin,
> They that breake word with heaven, will breake agen
> With all the world, and so thou doest with me.
>
> (3.1.69)

The actor playing the King might well get a laugh from these lines if he wants; but whether he does or not, the effect of the scene rests in its paradoxical distortions of the moment. A further complication is given to scene and characterization by Evadne's own admission that she loves "with my ambition / Not with my eies" and that she would abandon the King if ever he lost his throne. The King still cannot believe that Amintor could not sleep with Evadne and that he could bear the insult put upon him. Now, to clear herself, Evadne turns on Amintor, accusing him of sowing dissension between lovers, forcing him to acknowledge to the King that he knows the King is Evadne's lover. Shame forces him to threaten to draw his sword, but the King's command easily turns Amintor from this momentary defiance to an echo of *Hamlet*:

> but there is
> Divinitie about you, that strikes dead
> My rising passions; as you are my King,
> I fall before you and present my sword,
> To cut my owne flesh if it be your will. . . .
>
> (3.1.72)

The rising movement to action and the falling away is a familiar enough Fletcherian stage device. Amintor is pushed to the inevitable question and one crucial to any attempt to understand how he should be viewed:

> why did you choose out me
> To make thus wretched? there were thousands, fooles,
> Easie to worke on, and of state enough
> Within the Iland.
>
> (3.1.72)

But Evadne declares that she would never have a fool. Amintor suggests a hypocrite might have been picked, but the King assures him that he was chosen because he is as honest as he is valiant.

In short Amintor has been chosen the King's cuckold because of

his virtues. Surely we can take Amintor at this evaluation. Troubled,
confused, and inconsistent, he is not a fool, a coward, or a hypocrite.
The agony of his dilemma is increased by the paradox of his virtues.
Amintor himself recognizes the causal weight of his betrayal of
Aspatia—"This tis to breake a troth" (3.1.73). We recognize further
Amintor's confusion of reputation with honor, his uncomfortable
acceptance of the world of appearances. The scene is richly worked
for almost all possible emotional variations.

The link of *The Maid's Tragedy* with *Hamlet* is more than simply
a matter of an echo here and there. The parallels are pervasive and
varied in their effect, sometimes parodistic and at other times working to deepen the slighter material of *The Maid's Tragedy,* giving
it substance through association. Melantius would easily be recognized as Horatio to Amintor's Hamlet, a Horatio who takes on
Hamlet's task of revenge and who plays to his sister Evadne a
variation of Hamlet's scene to his mother. Amintor's pathetic cry—
"Thy love, o wretched I, thy love *Melantius,* / Why I have nothing
else"—might even be read to amplify and support Robert Ornstein's
perhaps not quite serious assertion that "Only Beaumont could have
'rewritten' *Hamlet* so as to make Horatio appear a latent homosexual."[7]

The scene in which Melantius brings Evadne to repentance and
convinces her to become the avenger of familial honor by killing
the King may gain additional substance and complexity through
the comparison with Hamlet's scene with his mother. Just how the
parallel with *Hamlet* would work depends finally on the playing of
the scene; an audience might be made to see Melantius and Evadne
parodically, their shallowness and the surface quality of their emotions unfavorably emphasized by the remembrance of the intensity
of emotions in *Hamlet.* Whatever interpretive ambiguities surround
the Evadne-Melantius scene, it is doubtless effectively constructed
to achieve the greatest stage effect.

The audience knows that the King is Evadne's lover and Melantius
knows it, but he pretends he does not and demands that she name
the "secure slave" (4.1.89). The only justification for Melantius's
pretense is theatrical. The naming of the King creates a climax and
effects a reprise of Evadne's admission to Amintor. When Evadne
comes to kill the King she will call him not by name (in fact he is
not given one) but by title. Throughout the play the title *King* is
used with musical effect as leitmotiv.

Evadne's repentance and her agreement to kill the King come

only after Melantius threatens to kill her. Such a swordpoint reformation is hardly convincing. Fletcher's concern is not with cre-
ating a convincing conversion but with a striking scene. Her stubborn
and spirited resistance, her complete reversal after Melantius's ter-
rifying threat, and her subsequent impassioned appeal to Amintor
for forgiveness are all milked for the greatest theatrical and rhetorical
advantage.

Evadne's murder of the King is brilliantly shaped, albeit annoying
to some critics for its perverse sexuality and unabashed sensationalism. It opens with a brief exchange with the gentleman guarding
the King's door. The light bawdry of the gentleman hits exactly
the saucy and improper tone a gentleman of the bed chamber might
take with the King's mistress—at least on stage. The shame of
Evadne's situation is deftly sketched here, but the gentleman's im-
proprieties will get a laugh against which Evadne's soliloquy sounds
strangely on the ears:

> The night grows horrible, and all about me
> Like my blacke purpose, O the conscience
> Of a lost virgin, whither wilt thou pull me?
> To what things dismall, as the depth of hell,
> Wilt thou provoke me?
>
>   (5.1.107)

All this is very fine, as is Evadne's resolve—recalling the scene when
Hamlet decides not to kill the King when he is praying lest he go
to heaven—but the innovative element in the scene comes when
Evadne ties the King to the bed and the newly awakened King takes
this for a delightful sexual game:

> What prettie new device is this *Evadne*?
> What, doe you tie me to you? by my love
> This is a queint one. . . .
>
>   (5.1.108)

What might have been a rather standard revenge murder has been
wittily transformed into an extravagant stage moment and an elaborate conceit:

Evadne.	I doe not mean Sir
	To part so fairely with you, we must change
	More of these love-trickes yet.
King.	What bloudie villaine
	Provok't thee to this murther?
Evadne.	Thou, thou monster. [*Stabs him.*]

Evadne's exit is followed by the entrance of two gentlemen of the bedchamber who return to the bawdy note struck by the gentleman at the opening of the scene: "Tis a fine wench, weele have a snap at her one of these nights as she goes from him" (5.1.111). The tone here brilliantly introduces the discovery of the murdered King. The tone, however, is less sure when Aspatia, disguised as a man, attempts to provoke Amintor at a fight and finally kicks him. It is difficult to see how a stage kick can be seriously given or that laughter is desirable at this point. Evadne, *"her hands bloudy with a knife,"* now tries to win Amintor's love and asks him to bed—at the very least a visually grotesque, if not downright perverse, scene.

The Maid's Tragedy never really achieves anything approaching tragic depth. The corpses at the end cannot move us because the characters have never convinced us. Aspatia has never been anything but the lovelorn maid, fated for a melodramatic last gasp. Evadne holds our interest but never our conviction. She is first the one-dimensional sexual villainess, then the wronged avenging maiden, and finally something like a pathetic lover. Amintor remains a puzzling character, but his complexity is on the surface and ultimately the consequence of the demands of plot and situation than of character. He is chosen the King's cuckold because he is loyal, honest, and eminently respectable. Melantius accepts Amintor's view of the divinity surrounding a king as reasonable and does not expect Amintor to work his own revenge.

With varying degrees of conviction *The Maid's Tragedy* does present an image of the court world with its concerns of love and honor and shifting views of kingship. The image in the mirror is sometimes strangely distorted, but never uninteresting. Whatever its weaknesses, *The Maid's Tragedy* is inventive and lively theater. That Edmund Waller revised it as a tragicomedy in the Restoration reflects the nature of the play—that is, its tendency to be tragicomedy—as much as the political expediency of avoiding offense to King Charles II.

Valentinian and *Bonduca*

The only two tragedies attributed to Fletcher working alone—
Valentinian and *Bonduca*—make use of Roman and Roman-British
materials. One need only cite Shakespeare's *Antony and Cleopatra*
(1608) and *Cymbeline* (1610) and Jonson's *Cataline* (1611) to illustrate
the popularity of Roman and Roman-British matter in the period.
Fletcher's interests in the materials, unlike Jonson's, are not historical, moral, or (except perhaps incidentally) political, but unabashedly theatrical.

The sources for *Valentinian* (1610–14) Fletcher found in the work
of the sixth-century historian Procopius and in the second part of
L'Honoré d'Urfé's lengthy French romance *L'Astrée,* published in
1610. Mincoff is undoubtedly correct in concluding "that Fletcher
was drawn to the story as he had read it in *L'Astrée,* that he turned
to an historical account in order to amplify it, and that finally he
built up the tragedy on the history rather than the romance."[8] In
Procopius and D'Urfé Fletcher found a satisfactorily lurid tale of
rape, murder, betrayal, and ambition set in the corrupt court of
crumbling imperial Rome.

The Emperor Valentinian satisfies his passion for Lucinda, the
virtuous wife of Maximus, by raping her. In the tradition of Lucrece,
Lucinda unhesitatingly responds to her ravishment and consequent
loss of her honor by committing suicide. (Procopius makes no such
report of Maximus's wife; but for the Renaissance stage suicide is
virtually an obligatory response to rape.) Maximus is now left with
the task of avenging his wife's dishonor and death. Certainly part
of Fletcher's attraction to the story lay in the opportunities for debate
over proper courses of action. Is suicide the correct response to a
rape? Does the woman, the victim, really lose her honor in a rape?
Is revenge the appropriate response? May a subject revenge himself
and his honor on his ruler?

Maximus's path to revenge is blocked by his friend, General
Aecius, a firm believer in the divine right of kings and consequently
absolutely loyal to the Emperor, no matter what his crimes. Maximus realizes that he cannot work his revenge on Emperor Valentinian until Aecius is destroyed. Another debate is joined here—
the obligations of friendship versus the demands of revenge. Maximus arouses the Emperor's suspicions against Aecius and arranges
his death.

The bawds charged with the murder of Aecius are too frightened even to attempt his assassination. Their replacement, Pontius, a former officer dismissed by Aecius, instead of being a resentful traitor, ready to murder his former commander, turns out to be exemplarily loyal. He demonstrates his loyalty and nobility of spirit by committing suicide and Aecius follows suit. Aecius's "bold and faithful Eunuchs," Phidius and Aretus, now avenge their master's death by poisoning Valentinian. Aretus makes the Emperor's final agonies all the more exquisite by taking the same poison two hours earlier so that Valentinian may have a preview of his death pains. Phidius completes this round of mortality by stabbing himself.

"Gods, what a sluce of blood have I let open!" (*DW*, vol. 4; 5.3.366), Maximus quite rightly declares. Unsatisfied with his revenge, he gives way to ambition, seeking and winning both the imperial throne and Valentinian's widow, Eudoxia. He overreaches himself, however, when he unwisely boasts to Eudoxia that he had Valentinian murdered to win her and even that he contrived in the rape of his wife. Eudoxia responds by poisoning him with the wreath with which he was crowned emperor.

The last three acts of *Valentinian* open with crisp and economical declarations of offstage action: act 3, "Tis done *Lycinius*" (the rape of Lucina); act 4, "Dead?" (Lucina's suicide); and act 5, "He h'as his last" (Valentinian has been given the fatal poison). These are fine dramatic strokes; but their classical restraint is at odds with the central interests of the play, which remain vivid, sensational, and broadly painted. Their contrast with the play's pervasive rhetorical flourishes and spectacular scenes suggests a work of light and shadow, of contrasts and qualifications that extend to theme and character.

Valentinian is another of those plays in which critics have sought to establish in Fletcher major thematic statements, even "his rabid propaganda of absolutism."[9] As the summary of the plot indicates, the action of the play obviously invites debates over both traditional themes and real concerns of the day. Lucina's rape and her immediate decision that she must preserve her own and her husband's honor prompt a discussion of that assumption. Aecius argues both that force removes the dishonor and that she should live in hopes of shaming Valentinian into reformation; he qualifies that argument, however, by suggesting that she live "a short year." Maximus rejects any compromise with honor, seeing no recourse for Lucina but suicide. The discussion provides conflict before the inevitable suicide, but the outcome is hardly an expression of Fletcher's own doctrine.

Valentinian is a revenge play, but that the rape to be avenged was perpetrated by a ruler provides an inevitable locus for debate over the propriety of killing wicked rulers. Aecius is a rigid absolutist who establishes his credentials early in the play:

> We are but subjects *Maximus;* obedience
> To what is done, and griefe for what is ill done,
> Is all we can call ours: the hearts of Princes
> Are like the Temples of the gods; pure incense
> Untill unhallowed hands defile those offrings,
> Burns ever there; we must not put 'em out,
> Because the Priests that touch those sweets are wicked;
> We dare not deerest friend. . . .
>
> (1.3.287)

Later, he tells Maximus that he would join him in revenge if the rapist had been anyone but the Emperor and argues against killing Valentinian on the more pragmatic grounds, rather than divine right, for to do so would threaten the state:

> were it not hazard
> And almost certaine losse of all the Empire,
> I would joyne with ye: were it any mans
> But his life, that is life of us, he lost it
> For doing of this mischiefe. . . .
>
> (3.3.334)

Aecius's royalism is extreme, but the issue is never debated in any depth. The point is less in the issue of loyalty to the Emperor than in the essential conflict between Aecius and Maximus, in the conflict of the absolutes of political loyalty and friendship. Both stand in the way of Maximus's revenge.

Phidias and Aretus, Aecius's loyal servants who poison Valentinian, obviously do not share their master's royalist scruples; nor does Eudoxia have any moral doubts about the propriety of murdering her new husband and emperor, Maximus. There is no reason to think any of these positions represented Fletcher's own views. Aecius's absolutist attitudes are used dramatically, not thematically or editorially.

Fletcher's use of his sources says a good deal about his conception of tragic drama. Instead of focusing on a major character and incidents relevant to that character, he uses virtually all the historical matter in order to produce a series of dramatic climaxes.

Valentinian is potentially a tragic character but not allowed to develop. His few redeeming moments are swallowed up by the corruption of his court, the gang of bawds that serve his lusts, and his own exuberant villainy:

> Come leave these lamentations, they doe nothing,
> But make a noyse: I am the same man still,
> Were it to doe again (therefore be wiser)
> By all this holy light, I should attempt it:
> Ye are so excellent, and made to ravish,
> (There were no pleasure in ye else). . . .
> (3.1.317)

His death scene is skillfully, almost lovingly, worked for the fullest dramatic effects. The Emperor is brought in on his chair with music and a song, "Care charming sleep, thou easer of all woes" (5.2.360).[10] Valentinian rages for drink to assuage the terrible thirst the poison has created while Aretus, dying of the same poison, cheerfully assures him that his agony will increase. Aretus dies and then Valentinian, calling out "I am mortal" (5.2.365), also expires. It is masterfully sensational.

By contrast, Aecius's death is a dramatic essay on the art of dying well:

> We must all die,
> All leave ourselves, it matters not, where, when,
> Nor how, so we die well: and can that man that does so
> Need lamentation for him?
> (4.4.347)

Valentinian's cowardly bawds run off merely at the sight of Aecius's drawn sword. Pontius, the centurion Aecius dismissed for speaking seditiously against Valentinian's corruption and decadence, now comes, Aecius assumes, to kill him on Valentinian's orders. Aecius

declares he will not resist Caesar's will in any way, that he holds
his sword only that he may die a soldier. But instead of killing
Aecius, Pontius kills himself to vindicate his honor.

Pontius's dying speech focuses on one of Fletcher's recurrent
themes—the deplorable softness of peace and the neglect of the
professional soldier in peacetime:

> If I were foe to any thing, t'was ease,
> Want of the Souldiers due, the Enemy;
> The nakednesse we found at home, and scorne,
> Children of peace, and pleasures; no regard
> Nor comfort for our scarres, but how we got 'em;
> To rusty time, that eate our bodies up,
> And even began to prey upon our honours;
> To wants at home, and more than wants, abuses;
> To them, that when the Enemy invaded,
> Made us their Saints, but now the sores of *Rome*;
> To silken flattery, and pride plumd over,
> Forgetting with what wind their feathers saile,
> And under whose protection their soft pleasures
> Grow full and numberlesse: to this I am foe,
> Not to the state, or any point of duty. . . .
>
> (4.4.352–53)

Pontius's espousal of heroic values, of war as a noble action anti-
thetical to the slothful and degenerative peace, is elegantly put, but
difficult to accept as anything more than a conceit to be enjoyed
for its own sake. The "Tommy Atkins" theme of the neglected
soldier in times of peace may have reflected some actual sympathy
for unemployed professional soldiers in London; but if we are to
take Pontius's remarks about peace seriously, this position contrasts
glaringly and insultingly with the views of King James, who prized
as "one of his favourite honorifics . . . *Rex Pacificus*."[11]

The death scenes provide high dramatic and rhetorical moments.
But their abundance underlines Fletcher's approach to the play as
a series of dramatic climaxes rather than a tragic whole. The audience, for example, is scarcely prepared for Maximus's complete
shift to villainy. Once his revenge is achieved he considers suicide
briefly (he can scarcely be blamed in so suicidal a play), but quickly
succumbs to ambition with an extraordinary line: "If I rise, / My
wife was ravished well" (5.3.82). Maximus's own death, poisoned

by his coronation wreath, is set within the pomp of the imperial
ceremony, complete with a procession, trumpets and hautboys, and
a heavily ironic song, "Honour that is ever living" (5.8.375).

   Valentinian presents broadly sketched characters and values, and
in Aecius and Pontius the honor of soldiers in the midst of courtly
corruption. In his dedicatory poem in the folio the Cavalier poet
Richard Lovelance singles out *Valentinian* to exemplify Fletcher's
tragedies:

> *And now thy purple-robed* Tragoedie,
> *In her embroider'd Buskins, calls mine eye,*
> *Where brave* Aecius *we see betray'd,*
> T'obey his Death, *whome thousand lives obey'd;*
> *Whilst that the* Mighty Foole *his Scepter breakes,*
> *And through his* Gen'rals *wounds his owne doome speaks,*
> *Weaving thus richly* Valentinian
> *The costliest Monarch with the cheapest man.*
>
> (Folio, B2v)

Lovelace's lines stress the sharp contrasts of the play, the baroque
delight in chiaroscuro. Questions of honor, duty, and political limits
provide moments of debate, heroics, and stage excitement. Public
characters ask public questions, and their public answers yield a
bloody public spectacle at a substantial remove from any private
realities.

   Bonduca (1611–14) was not surprisingly adapted as an opera in
1696 by George Powell.[12] It is operatic in nature, filled with considerable spectacle, songs, drums and trumpets, and rhetorical set
pieces. The stage directions for the opening of act 3, for example,
call for music and then: *"Enter in Solemnity, the Druids singing, the*
second daughter *strewing flowers: then* Bonduca, [first Daughter],
Caratach, Nennius, *and others"* (*DW,* vol. 4; 3.1.191).

   Such moments of spectacle go some way to make up for the lack
of plot development and character interest. *Bonduca* is a tragedy
because of its deaths. Bonduca, who is the British heroine more
familiarly known as Boadicea, along with her two daughters, commits suicide after the British are defeated; and Ponius, a Roman
officer, kills himself in shame at his dereliction of duty. The brave
British boy Hengo, nephew of the hero Caratach, is treacherously
slain by the Romans. This is a modest enough casualty list; more
importantly, none of these characters is developed as a tragic pro-

tagonist. *Bonduca* is more precisely a history play—albeit a loosely structured one—than a tragedy, but it is no more truly historical than *Cymbeline,* to which it is very distantly related. Both plays, of course, use Roman-British material. Perhaps *Bonduca* is best described as heroic drama because the play considers themes—honor, courage—appropriate to that genre. Indeed, one critic argues that *Bonduca* is "Essentially a drama of ideas . . . [which] develops a code of ethics for the heroic life."[13]

"Ideas" seems a rather strong word for *Bonduca,* implying the presence of serious doctrine of some sort. "Rhetorical stances" may more accurately reflect the nature of the play. *Bonduca* opens with what amounts to a debate on the good manners appropriate to a victor. Bonduca boasts in a most vulgar fashion of her victory over the Romans: "A woman beat 'em, *Nennius*; a weak woman, / A woman beat these *Romanes*" (1.1.157). This earns Caratach's sharp rebuke: "So it seems. / A man would shame to talk so" (1.1.157). Caratach goes on (at length) to lecture Bonduca on respect for the courage of the Roman enemy:

> I love an enemy: I was born a souldier;
> And he that in the head on's Troop defies me,
> Bending my manly body with his sword,
> I make a Mistris.
>
>   (1.1.159)

The mannered lecture on manners, the conceit of the enemy as a mistress, are odd enough qualifications of the heroic vein, but the heroics of the play are more stage moments than a consistent tone. Comedy is supplied by the lovesick officer Junius, in love with Bonduca's younger daughter, and by Corporal Judas and his companions, hungry knaves all. Junius's lovesickness and the antics of the hungry knaves, however, both provide the sententious Caratach with opportunities to demonstrate and speak on magnanimity to enemies.

The hungry knaves are captured by the British when foraging for food. Bonduca's daughters, vengeful because they both were raped by the Romans, are ready to hang Corporal Judas and his fellows. Caratach instead orders the soldiers fed and supplied with enough wine to provide tipsy comedy. When Bonduca's daughters manage to capture Junius with a false letter, Caratach chides them for their

treachery and bloody-mindedness. He responds most unsympath-
etically to the second daughter's assertion that they must revenge
their rapes—"You should have kept your legs close then" (3.5.202)—
and orders Junius and his companions released.

Caratach's concern with honor is balanced by the nobility of the
Roman commander, Swetonius; the British and the Romans are
equal in the proper understanding of true heroic action. The theme
of honor is further developed in the character of Penius, a proud
and touchy officer who refuses Swetonius's order to join his regiment
to the battle. "Must come up? / Am I turn'd bare Centurion?"
(2.1.173). Penius's pride is coupled with a sense that the very
numbers of the Britons make combat unwise. Given a certain distance, Penius recalls Shakespeare's Enobarbus in *Anthony and Cleopatra* in his eventual mortifying shame and in the opportunity he
provides Swetonius for magnanimous behavior. After the Roman
victory Swetonius sends Petillius to forgive Penius. In one of those
switches Fletcher so enjoyed Petillius begins by urging Penius not
to commit suicide and ends by agreeing that suicide is actually the
proper step.

As the foregoing should make clear, *Bonduca* is weakly plotted
and highly episodic. The suicides of Bonduca and her daughters
and of Penius are theatrical highpoints, but without much ultimate
significance. Hengo, the brave little boy, is given an heroic and
pathetic death, which Algernon Charles Swinburne at least found
"a scene which of itself would have suffered to enroll [Fletcher's]
name forever on the list of our great tragic poets,"[14] a view more
likely to be shared in 1910 than currently. Penius and Hengo have
retreated to a rock, presumably the balcony above the stage, when
the body of Penius is brought by. Caratach stops the funeral cortege
and delivers a eulogy on Penius's virtues. Language and spectacle,
then, take precedence over plot and character. At the end of the
play Hengo's pathetic death is countered by the honorable surrender
of Caratach. Swetonius's last words—"March on, and through the
Camp in every tongue, / The Vertues of great *Caratach* be sung"
(5.3.244)—affirm a world in which the heroic and the honorable
have displaced the tragic.

Finally, *Bonduca* has about it the feeling of the jerry-built or the
prefabricated. It is theatrically competent. Varied scene and action,
an abundance of martial music and noise, pathos and rhetoric insure
the audience's interest. It is not a dull play, but it does confirm

our sense that Fletcher's heart was not in tragedy. The comedy of the lovesick Junius and the farcical doings of Corporal Judas, that hungry rogue, are easily as memorable as Bonduca's suicide and Hengo's death.

Collaborative Tragedies

Thierry and Theodoret (1607–21) is a collaborative work credited to Beaumont, Fletcher, and Philip Massinger. Fletcher's share is generally accepted as 1.1, 2.2–3, 4.1, and 5.2. The dating is uncertain, but Fletcher's collaboration with Massinger began in 1616, indicating a revision of the play after that date. It was published in quarto in 1621.

Thierry and Theodoret is a wild and woolly play, packed with sensational materials: a corrupt lecherous queen mother, an effective anaphrodisiac to spoil a royal wedding night, a plot to work a sacrificial murder, two royal assassinations—one by stabbing, the other by a poisoned handkerchief that keeps the victim's eyes open until he dies from lack of sleep. The play reverses the *Lear* situation with a thoroughly wicked mother and two fairly decent brothers in place of a decent, if confused, king and two wicked sisters.

The play's opening scene, by Fletcher, also recalls Hamlet with his mother as Theodoret, Prince of Austrachia, chides his mother, Queen Brunhalt, for her unchaste behavior, "her guilded knaves, brokers, and bedders" (*DW*, vol. 3; 1.1.379) and in particular her lover Protaldye. Brunhalt, unlike Gertrude, Hamlet's mother, is furious at being so corrected and resolves, as a perverse Lear, to go to her son Thierry, King of France, who will be sympathetic to her complaints against Theodoret.

Brunhalt is a complete villainess, a monster of lust and self-will. Fletcher opens the play with powerful images of corrupt sexuality. "Must I be chast *Protaldye?*" she cries and his response is kisses. "I live honest? / He may as well bid dead men walke; I humbled / Or bent below my power? let night dogs tear me" (1.1.382). But the scene and Brunhalt herself are not without a note of grotesque, burlesque comedy. Brunhalt rounds on a comment by Lecure, one of her gang of panders: "What's that to you, or any / Yee dosse, you powdered pigsbones, rubarbe glister?" Fletcher's sexy villainess is also a comic fishwife.

Brunhalt's intention is to turn Thierry against his brother, but to her surprise and discomfiture Theodoret arrives in Thierry's court and makes peace with him. Brunhalt is further disturbed with the arrival of Thierry's betrothed Ordella. She feels her power slipping from her. Lecure promises to supply her with an anaphrodisiac that will render Thierry impotent and Ordella so disappointed that she will demand the marriage be annulled. This expository matter by Massinger is followed by comic business by Fletcher in which Protaldye's cowardice is graphically demonstrated as he submits to a farcical kicking.

Massinger is credited with the court scenes in which Protaldye's disgrace is made public, much to Brunhalt's anger, and Thierry is given the antilove potion. The act ends with Brunhalt calling Protaldye to bed and vowing Theodoret's death, "For he's the engin usde to ruine us" (2.4.409). Brunhalt's motives are no more complex than this.

Linguistic analysis credits Beaumont with act 3. It opens with a sensational postmarriage night scene with Thierry and Ordella "as from bed." In a variation on the similar scene in *The Maid's Tragedy*, Ordella sweetly forgives Thierry his impotency. Brunhalt lays the next trap for Thierry by sending him to a "learned astronomer" for a cure. There is more comic business with the cowardice of Protaldye and high drama when Theodoret is stabbed by Protaldye from behind the state curtain. Brunhalt dissuades Thierry from burning down the palace to flush out the murderer by claiming that Theodoret really was not her son after all, but a gardener's baby substituted after a miscarriage. Thierry accepts this flimsy device without hesitation and turns to a more major concern—overcoming his impotency. He consults Lecure, now in disguise as the wise astrologer, and is told that he can recover if the first woman he sees coming out of Diana's temple is sacrificed (recalling the story of Jephthah, the ballad Hamlet remembers and the situation in *The Mad Lover* in which the princess is to marry the first man she sees coming from the temple of Venus). In a bound the action has moved to the realm of romance.

Brunhalt's agent, Lecure, has, of course, arranged that the first lady to come out of the temple is the veiled Ordella. The scene is Fletcher's; and he works it to the fullest emotional and rhetorical potential. But it is also comic. Thierry and his noble kinsman, Martell, wait outside the temple for the first woman to come out. Two men exit, "The plagues of men light on um, / They crosse my hopes like hares." A priest comes out. "Would he were gelt" Thierry remarks. "May not these rascalls serve Sir, / Well hang'd and quarter'd?" (4.1.426). The comedy is slight, hardly worth remarking, except that it is so typical of Fletcher and his dramatic sense. He deliberately creates a comic moment; he writes in some obvious laughs not only, surely, to intensify the emotionalism of Ordella's entrance by the contrast, but also because the romance world of the moment is first and foremost theatrical and Fletcher above all an entertainer.

Thierry's question—is she willing to die for king and kingdom?—produces two balanced pictures of death, Thierry's dark portrait and Ordella's eloquent dismissal of its fears:

> 'Tis of all sleepes the sweetest,
> Children begin it to us, strong men seeke it,
> And, kings from heigth of all their painted glories
> Fall, like spent exhalations, to this center;
> And those are fooles that feare it, or imagine
> A few unhandsome pleasures, or lifes profits
> Can recompence this place; and mad that staies it,
> Till age blow out their lights, or rotten humors
> Bring um despers'd to the earth.
>
> (4.1.428–29)

The passage brilliantly reminds us of Fletcher's poetic strengths.

The dramatic climax is reached when Thierry, sword drawn, and prepared to kill Ordella, removes her veil and recognizes her as his wife. It is another mark of Fletcher's dramatic sense that he gives Thierry only a four-line response and allows him to rush off the stage. The rest of the scene is played between Ordella and Martell and reaches a second climactic moment when Ordella draws a knife and offers to commit suicide. Martell discourages her and turns the plot against Brunhalt by declaring that he will report Ordella's death in hopes of getting the Queen to reveal her complicity in the machinations against Thierry and Ordella. The scene bears more than linguistic marks of Fletcher's skilled hand.

Massinger now takes over. Martell (falsely) reports Ordella's suicide. Thierry resolves to follow her last command to produce a daughter to carry her name. Memberge, Theodoret's daughter, enters to plead justice for her father's death. Theodoret proposes to marry her, forcing Brunhalt to avert an incestuous match by re-

112

vealing that she lied about Theodoret and that he was indeed her son. Her villainy clear to all, Brunhalt now gives Thierry the poisoned handkerchief to wipe his tears.

The denouement begins with a comic scene in Beaumont's hand in which Captain Devitry teaches his poor soldiers to rob rather than to beg. Their victim is the despicable Protaldye from whom they take a letter revealing the fullness of Brunhalt's and his treason. Fletcher begins the last scene with the aptly named Bawdber comically reporting on the failure of various physicians to cure Thierry. Thierry, now dying of sleeplessness, is carried in on a bed. Martell, Devitry, and a few soldiers bring in Brunhalt who is being appropriately tortured by being kept awake. Thierry's pathetic wonder at his mother's cruelty and his continued dutiful love leave Brunhalt totally unmoved and unrepentant: "if there be new curses in old nature, / I have a soule dare send um" (5.2.454).

The monstrous lady is carted off to be kept awake some more and to watch her lover Protaldye being broken on the wheel. Ordella now arrives for reunion with Thierry. The revelation that she lives provides another emotional peak to the scene, a kiss, and a final disposition of the kingdom to Martell and Memberge. But now both Thierry and Ordella die. Ordella dies, presumably, of dramatic symmetry; no cause is given, but surely none is needed.

"This is," Clifford Leech remarks, "a plot to dull the sensibilities"[15] but not a dull plot or a dull play. The action flows out of Brunhalt's natural and unmotivated malignity. She, her bawds, and her lover are grotesques; she herself moves in a twilight world of comedy and true evil. For all that the part is a fine and demanding role; she ranks high among Fletcher's depraved women.

None of the characters is to be taken or can be taken with any seriousness. Thierry believes his brother is the gardener's son when Brunhalt tells him so and as easily accepts her recantation. The murder of Theodoret fails to concern him because the plot demands that it not. If Theodoret were to survive being stabbed, Brunhalt repent at the sight of Thierry's sleepless agony and produce an antidote, no harm would be done, least of all to the fabric of the play. Tragedy would become tragicomedy, but the essentials, the mood, the tone, and the dramatic feel of the play would not have been changed. In the scenes attributed to Fletcher his craftsmanship is sure and of a piece with his unaided work, but *Thierry and Theodoret* also shows the collaborative skill that has entertainment as its primary goal.

Rollo, Duke of Normandy; or, The Bloody Brother (1616–24) was first printed in quarto in 1639. The work of George Chapman, Massinger, Fletcher, and probably Ben Jonson, it achieved considerable popularity, and performances are frequently mentioned in seventeenth-century theatrical annals. Its source is in Roman history, but the action has been transferred to a nonhistorical Normandy.[16] Rollo and Otto are joint inheritors of the dukedom. They do not, however, share their inheritance easily. Rollo at first attempts to poison Otto, but Otto refuses to partake of the poisoned banquet prepared for him. Rollo is then forced to kill his brother with his own hands; the murder accomplished, he launches on a tyrannical and murderous reign. Such is his savagery that he scolds his henchman for beheading one victim with an ax and orders the next head cut off with a sword because it is crueller.

Rollo is a complete villain, but there is room in his heart to fall in love with the daughter of one of his victims. Edith, although almost sweet-talked out of her revenge, aids and abets in Rollo's assassination by the brother of another victim. *The Bloody Brother* offers melodramatic evil, a villain's role, some high rhetoric, and some debate on the popular stage question of how to deal with vicious rulers, all mixed with some effective stage comedy and a few songs.

Fletcher contributes the comedy of the kitchen staff who are so easily turned poisoners, and a rollicking scene (before they are taken off to be hanged) in which they sing sprightly hanging ballads. Fletcher may also have written the second stanza to the song "Take, Oh take those lips away" borrowed from Shakespeare's *Measure for Measure* for the courting scene in the fifth act of Rollo and Edith beginning "Hide, Oh hide those hills of Snow" (*W*, vol. 4; 5.2.307). Fletcher is responsible for most of the last act, and he manages to give it one of those dramatic turns at which he was so skilled. Edith is resolved to revenge her father's death. The wicked Rollo, however, becomes so eloquent in his expression of love that Edith is nearly won over. Rollo takes the familiar conceit of killing eyes, most appropriate for the would-be avenger, and so argues that Edith must pray in a breathy aside, "Now heaven thy help, or I am gone for ever, / His tongue has turn'd me into melting pity" (5.2.309). On

these lines Rollo's executioner makes a timely entrance. The twist
adds an unexpected moment of suspense to the scene and affirms
Fletcher's easy control of dramatic devices. *The Bloody Brother* has
no psychological depth, no real tragic dimensions, but it is an
impressive example of the kind of surefire entertainment the professional playwrights of the day could put together with apparent ease
and theatrical efficiency.

Sir John Van Olden Barnavelt (1619) provides an even more striking
example of Fletcher, this time working with Massinger alone, turning out a play to meet an immediate topical interest. In May 1619
the Dutch statesman John Van Oldenbarneveldt was executed on a
charge of treason. Oldenbarneveldt's execution was of interest both
because of his political importance and because of his connections
with the more liberal Calvinists known as Arminians. On 14 August
1619 Thomas Locke wrote to Sir Dudley Carleton, the English
ambassador at The Hague: "The Players heere were bringing of
Barnavelt upon the stage, and had bestowed a great deale of money
to prepare all things for the purpose, but at th' instant were pro-
hibited by my Lo: of London." The objections of the bishop of
London were overcome, and by 27 August Locke reported to Carleton that "Our players have fownd the meanes to go through with
the play of Barnavelt, and it hath many spectators and received
applause."[17]

Even though a quarto publication of a play of such topical interest
might be expected, *Sir John Van Olden Barnavelt* was not published
until the nineteenth century. The play exists in a manuscript in the
hand of the scrivener Ralph Crane, with additions in the hands of
the prompter and of Sir George Buc, the master of the revels, who
censored the manuscript prior to performance. At one point Buc,
ever mindful of royal prerogatives, has written, "I like not this:
neithr do I think yt the prince was thus disgracefully used. besides
he is to much presented."[18]

Today's equivalent of *Sir John Van Olden Barnavelt* would be the
television documentary drama. Fletcher and Massinger quickly produced a play on a much discussed item of international news. Barnavelt was a figure of towering importance in the Netherlands. His
execution would have been the subject of universal conversation.
The collaborators make no real attempt at a deep analysis of Barnavelt's fall or his character. He is treated conventionally as an arrogant man driven by his overweening ambition to challenge the

rule of the prince of Orange. Although the humanist and jurist, Hugo Grotius, and others connected with Arminian theology are presented on the stage, Fletcher and Massinger do not deal with the issues of the Arminian controversy; in fact, in one of the comic scenes an English lady mocks two Dutch women for their Arminian beliefs in the broadest fashion.

The collaborators are not, then, concerned with presenting an intellectual study of Barnavelt and the issues surrounding his execution. Instead they are most interested in the opportunities for playing the sensational, the rhetorical, and in adding the requisite amount of comedy.

The Dutch women in the scene just alluded to are bossy and masculine, reminiscent of the "ladies collegiate" in Ben Jonson's *Epicoene*. The English woman rebukes them with the observation that "our Cuntry brings us up to faire obedience, / to know our husbands for our Governors" (2.2.26). One of Barnavelt's confederates, Leidenbergh, committed suicide while in prison and in the presence of his son who had been allowed to act as his servant. Massinger writes the scene for all its potential pathos. When Barnavelt is executed Leidenburgh's coffin is hung from the gallows, a sensational macabre touch calling up some grotesque commentary from the executioner:

> a plaguy heavy lubber: sure this fellow
> ha's a bushhell of plot in's belly, he waighes so massy:
> heigh: now againe: he stincks, like a hung poll cat
> this rotten treason has a vengaunce savor.
> this venison wants pepper, and salt abhominably.
> (5.3.88)

More gallows humor is supplied when the executioners of Harlem, Utrecht, and Leiden throw dice to see who will have the honor of executing Barnavelt. The festive nature of the scene is confirmed with a song.

As a tragedy *Sir John Van Olden Barnavelt* lacks force and a real tragic center. Considered as a piece of current history quickly written to take advantage of current interest it is effective entertainment.

If *Sir John Van Olden Barnavelt* is a television docudrama, *The Double Marriage* (1619–23) is a Saturday morning cartoon. Fletcher and Massinger, again working in collaboration, draw on Thomas

Danett's translation of *The Historie of Philip De Commines* (1596), Lazarus Pyott's *The Orator,* and part 1 of Cervantes's *Don Quixote,* as well as the *Controversiae* of Seneca the Elder.

In the opening scene, recalling *Julius Caesar,* Virolet explains to his concerned wife, Juliana, that his absence from his bed is the consequence of his plotting a rebellion against the terrible Neapolitan tyrant, Ferrand, a ruler so wicked that he even sold the "Bishoprick of *Tarent* to a Jew" (*W,* vol. 6; 1.1.325). His coconspirators make the mistake of including Ferrand's villainous aide, Ronvere, in their plot. But he betrays them and all are arrested save Virolet, who manages to go into hiding. Ferrand, in a nicely sensational scene, probably by Massinger, tortures Juliana on a rack to force her to reveal Virolet's whereabouts. Juliana heroically refuses to betray her husband. Ferrand pretends to be so impressed that he releases her and pardons the rebels on condition that Virolet take charge of the campaign against his archenemy, the pirate Duke of Sesse, who has captured his nephew and heir to the throne, Ascanio.

The second act, written by Fletcher, takes place at sea aboard the pirate ship. The Duke of Sesse is one of those noble pirates of romance with a beautiful and warlike daughter, Martia, and a virtuous hatred for the tyrannical Ferrand. Virolet's ship engages Sesse's in battle but he and his crew are taken by the pirates. Virolet is chained with Ascanio, but not for long. Martia falls in love with him and declares that she will release him and Ascanio if Virolet will marry her. She brushes aside his objections that he is already married and he agrees to marry her, establishing the dilemma of the title. Their escape in a longboat is accompanied with a substantial firing of stage cannon. The scene is one of pure romance. Momentarily Sesse and his daughter even call to mind Prospero and Miranda, father and daughter exiled by a wicked world.

Sesse's Boatswain and Gunner are bluff, rough and ready characters, loyal and jolly. Boys scramble up rigging, the pirates rush about dealing with the enemy, trumpets sound, and cannon roar. It is all lively and noisy, with no pretensions beyond the attention such devices can evoke.

The action quickly shifts back to Naples. Virolet acknowledges his new marriage to Juliana who bears the shock with heroic nobility and undiminished love for her husband. Virolet refuses to consummate his marriage with Martia. This denial infuriates Martia who revenges herself by becoming mistress of the tyrant Ferrand. The

Duke of Sesse meanwhile has landed at Naples in pursuit of his runaway daughter and revenge. He leads the citizens in rebellion. Juliana stabs Virolet to death by mistake when he is disguised, for not very convincing reasons, as the villain Ronvere. Virolet's reaction is a predictable conceit:

> O courteous hand, nay thou has done most nobly,
> And heaven has guided thee, 'twas their great justice;
> O blessed wound that I could come to kiss thee!
> How beautiful and sweet thou shew'st!"
>
> (5.2.397)

Juliana in her grief sits beside the corpse of her beloved and sometime husband. When the pageboy picks her up he finds her "cold and stiff / Stiff as a stake, she's dead" (5.2.400). *Rigor mortis* comes quickly on the Fletcherian stage, but not before Ferrand is beheaded and the Boatswain kills Martia, a courteous act to keep her father from the shame of having to kill his own daughter. Ascanio is declared the new King of Naples. Ronvere is somehow forgotten in the general carnage, perhaps a casualty to the vagaries of collaboration or just to general haste of composition, but his corpse is not greatly missed.

The Double Marriage is a potboiler and that fact may be the most interesting thing about the play. It is another reminder of the demands placed on the playwright to keep the stage supplied with material. It is a thoroughly workmanlike drama of adventure filled with action and a dramatic moral dilemma in the problem of Virolet's double marriage. The authors do not care about the possible ethical considerations; legalistic debate does not interest them here, but the potential for pathos does. Most significantly *The Double Marriage* is a tragedy only by reason of the corpses. In spirit and feeling it belongs to the realm of tragicomic romance. Characters are pasteboard figures capable of rant and pathos; there is no tragic idea or theme. A good portion of the stage action is filled with virtually freestanding comedy. It was played at court in 1687, and that at least should be testimony to its surviving power as an entertainment.

Fletcher's view of tragedy is essentially that it means deaths. It may not be unfair to say that he subscribed to a cumulative vision of tragedy—the more numerous the deaths, the more greatly tragic.

Character and the relation of character to the events of tragedy are not substantial concerns. The tragedies do not aspire to philosophical dimensions. By and large the tragedies really want to be tragicomedies in the sense that if the deaths were averted the world of these plays would be identical in feeling and tone to that of the tragicomedies.

We never come away deeply moved by a Fletcherian tragedy, but we can feel well entertained. The audience will be touched by individual speeches, by high rhetoric, by moments of real poetry, by telling scenes, but not by the total effect of any one of the tragedies. The entertainment is not simply in the variety and ingenuity of scenes, in the clever mix of tones and styles—tragic, tragicomic, romantic, and comic—but in the enjoyment of the pure professional skill demonstrated in the plays. Fletcher's generic modes are tragicomedy and, above all, comedy. As a writer of tragedies we admire not his tragic but his theatrical sense.

Chapter Five

"Mirth with Rosie Wings": The Comedies

The Comic Reach

Absolute accuracy about the canon of John Fletcher's plays is clearly an impossibility. Uncertainties of attribution are unlikely ever to be totally resolved. Consequently, if we say that 47 percent of Fletcher's plays were comedies, a cautionary "about" must be added, especially when we consider that the distinction between comedy and tragicomedy is not always to be made with ease. The genres slide about in their categorical boxes, and Fletcher himself, as we have seen, delighted in dramatic mixes and contrasts.

Nonetheless, if the precision of a percentage must be hedged, it is possible to say with assurance that almost half of Fletcher's plays, written either alone or in collaboration, were comedies. Moreover, the purely comic scenes in the tragicomedies and the tragedies make clear both Fletcher's skill and delight in writing comedy. He wrote in the comic vein throughout his career and has a major status as a comic writer. If Fletcher is not to be ranked with Congreve and Shaw as a master of the comic mode and writer of great comedies, he is at least a master of the comic moment, a creator of brilliant comic scenes and of a set of stageworthy comic characters, from wits to grotesques, and of a rich and varied comic language, including and extending beyond that "conversation of gentlemen" John Dryden so admired.

Many of the comic patterns, themes, and character types found in Fletcher's comedies have already been seen in that group of comedies associated with the boys' companies. A distinction that separates these comedies from the rest of the comic plays is artificial, and almost any attempt at classification of the other comedies shares that artificiality and arbitrariness. "The War of the Sexes" is certainly a major topic that might be applied to a grouping of plays. The trouble is that the grouping is too large and, indeed, the subject is present in almost all the comedies. "Plays of Wit and Folly," "Wit, Folly, and Romance," "Farce and Romance," or "Romance, Wit, Humours" Polonius-like all suggest themselves until the inevitable is accepted. Fletcher's style and subject matter is as mixed in the comedies as it is elsewhere.

The simplest division of the comedies into those attributed to Fletcher alone and those written collaboratively perhaps allows for the most certainty in locating Fletcher's own comic genius. Such a division results in a tally of eight comedies by Fletcher alone and ten collaborative works (excluding those discussed earlier). There are obviously too many comedies to discuss them all, but division by authorship allows for concentration on the best of the works and reinforces our perception of both their internal variety and their external similarities.

Fletcher Alone

The plays written alone will be examined in varying detail, some much more briefly than others. The first of these, *The Woman's Prize, or The Tamer Tamed*, written possibly as early as 1604 and acted in 1611, is a spin-off from Shakespeare's *Taming of the Shrew* and an echo of the Aristophanic battle of the sexes.

The action has been transferred from Padua to London, where the widowed Petruchio has wed a new wife, Maria. Maria, however, has no intention of undergoing the trials and taming endured by her matrimonial predecessor. Instead she resolves to tame Petruchio. Maria's plan, recalling *Lysistrata*, is to deny Petruchio sexual comfort until he grants her sexual equality. The tiring house becomes a site for siege when the women lock themselves up. "The chamber's nothing but a meere *Ostend*, in every window Pewter cannons mounted, you'l quickly finde with what they are charg'd, sir"[1] (*DW*, vol. 4; 1.3.31). The cannon are chamber pots and the siege scenes are the occasion for lively farcical action that includes a gaggle of boisterous city and country wives singing:

> A health for all this day
> To the woman that bears the sway
> And wears the breeches;
> Let it come, let it come.
>
> (2.6.54)

These harridans serve to counterbalance any view that Fletcher was greatly serious about the rights of women, as does the romantic subplot in which Livia, a romantic heroine, joins the rebel ladies only to save herself from marriage to old Morose and to trick him and her father into consenting to her marriage with her true love. Petruchio is tamed, but the social fabric is hardly threatened; and no opportunity for traditional comic antifeminine rant and roaring is lost. The battle of the sexes in *The Woman's Prize* is ultimately a draw.

The Night Walker, or The Little Thief (1611–14) was revised by James Shirley and licensed in May 1633. Samuel Pepys saw three performances and enjoyed each one. In 1691 the theatrical writer Gerard Langbaine described it as still popular and frequently acted.[2] Its popularity is understandable and well deserved, for it is a bouncy and entertaining farrago of romance, farce, wit and gulling, mistaken identities (including a supposed ghost), and happy absurdities.

Tom Lurcher and Jack Wildbrain, two irresponsible and irrepressible gentlemen hell-raisers, generate the major plot lines along with the romantic male lead, Frank Hartlove. Lurcher and Wildbrain confirm Cyrus Hoy's observation that "The first thing to be noted about Fletcherian comedy is the presence, at the center of the comic design, of a lively, uninhibited and highly resolute young male character or characters (often they come in pairs) who mastermind the amorous and/or monetary rewards which accompany the plot's successful resolution."[3]

Lurcher has lost his property to the old and villainous usurer Algripe and has happily taken to theft to support himself. A bright and lively boy, who turns out to be Lurcher's sister, comes to assist him in his felonious activities. In the romantic plot Frank Hartwell's love Maria is forced by her greedy mother to marry the rich old usurer Algripe. Wildbrain attempts to prevent consummation of the marriage by encouraging Hartlove to attempt to seduce Maria before she is bedded by Algripe and then revealing them in an apparently compromising situation. Maria, a model of propriety, is so shocked by this insult to her honor that she falls into a deep swoon, so deep that she is taken for dead. When Lurcher and the "Boy" attempt to rob the house, they mistake Maria's coffin for the jewel chest and carry it away. In the course of their attempt to bury the coffin, Maria recovers, lending her apparently ghostly presence to the action.

Further complications include Wildbrain's involvement with Lurcher's mistress, a duel, a bell-ringing scene in which Lurcher revenges himself by stealing Wildbrain's clothes, and Maria's disguise as a Welsh maid who wins Hartlove's heart. Algripe is brought to repentence when "two Furies, with black Tapers" (*W,* vol. 7; 4.1.364) threaten to tear apart this prototypical Scrooge. The Boy, in the guise of an angel, comes to his rescue. Algripe confesses to cheating Lurcher and admits his prior contract to Lurcher's sister, Alanthe, "the little thief." Hartlove and Maria may now marry, Lurcher is restored to his fortune, Wildbrain to the favor of his rich aunt, and even "the little thief" seems happy at the prospect of her union with the reformed usurer.

Probability, obviously, is not the strong suit of *The Night Walker,* but the objection hardly arises in the midst of so much and so varied action. Maria, her close scrape with an enforced marriage and her presumed death, recalls Juliet: "A sad wedding / Her grave must be her Bridal bed" (1.2.326). Her nurse, although not as major as her counterpart in *Romeo and Juliet,* is capable of some vigorous bawdry. In her disguise as the Welsh girl, however, Maria adds a degree of comic wit to the romantic role. Much of the play takes place in the dark with all the opportunities for mistakes, surprises, and frights it offers. The boy wearing a false beard and riding on Lurcher's shoulders terrifies the servant/clown Tobie as the ghost of one of the guard: "Sure he farts fire . . . / Out with thy Prayerbook Nurse." To which the Nurse replies with stunning absurdity: "It fell ith' frying pan, and the Cat's eat it" (2.1.329). The action of *The Night Walker* is as free and exuberant as the language.

Wit Without Money (1614–20) is not so wild a play, but in its hero, Valentine, Fletcher creates another witty and willful masculine hero and a variation on the impoverished young gentleman theme. Valentine has squandered his means, but the merchant who holds the mortgage is not an Algripe and stands ready to return it to Valentine if he would only take some sensible steps to restore his fortune—in particular, marry a rich widow. Valentine, however, is not simply a spendthrift, but an eccentric with a doctrine that places wit above estate management, "holding it monstrous, men should feed their bodies, and starve their understandings" (*W,* vol. 2; 1.1.146). With a fine contempt, recalling Volpone, he rejects the labors and concerns of the landed gentry and boasts of his freedom and the merit of his landless state: "How bravely now I live, how jocund, how near the first inheritance, without fears, how free from title-troubles!"[4] (1.1.151).

Valentine's confidence in the economic power of his wit is reinforced by the arrival of servants bringing him a new hat and cloak and gold from his clients, the three suitors of the rich widow, Lady Hartwell. Valentine has become a consultant in widow-hunting. Like Iago, his conception is to "make my fool my purse." In the usual game of chase-the-widow the penniless, witty intriguer stalks a bride and a fortune. In *Wit Without Money* Valentine varies the plot by directing his wit at gulling the fortune-hunting suitors instead of trying to win the widow. Valentine, moreover, outrageously rejects the very concept of marrying widows: "they that enjoy 'em, lie but with dead men's monuments, and beget only their own ill Epitaphs . . ." (2.1.157).

Valentine's misogyny results in a witty essay on the woes of marriage:

why 'tis a monstrous thing to marry at all, especially as now 'tis made; me thinks a man, an understanding man, is more wise to me, and of a nobler tie, than all these trinkets; what do we get by women, but our senses, which is the rankest part about us, satisfied, and when that's done, what are we? Crest-fallen Cowards. What benefit can children be, but charges and disobedience? What's the love they render at one and twenty years? I pray die Father: when they are young, they are like bells rung backwards, nothing but noise and giddiness; and come to years once, there drops a son by th' sword in his Mistresses quarrel, a great joy to his parents: A Daughter ripe too, grows high and lusty in her blood, must have a heating, runs away with a supple ham'd Servingman: his twenty Nobles spent, takes to a trade, and learns to spin mens hair off; there's another, and most are of this nature. . . ." (2.1.158)

The prose in its vigorous rhythms reaches toward verse and exemplifies in its biting wit and easy urbanity the authority of Fletcher's comic voice. Valentine's masculine hubris, here so unqualifiedly established, moreover, delightfully sets the terms of the battle of the sexes when he meets his feminine match in the feisty Lady Hartwell, who gives as good as she gets and perhaps better:

You are no Whoremasters? Alas, no, Gentlemen, it were an impudence to think you vicious: you are so holy handsome Ladies fright you, you are the cool things of the time, the temperance, meer Emblems of the Law,

and veils of Vertue, you are not daily mending like Dutch Watches, and
plastering like old Walls; they are not Gentlemen, that with their secret
sins increase our Surgeons, and lie in Foraign Countries, for new sores;
Women are all these Vices; you are not envious, false, covetous, vainglorious, irreligious, drunken, revengeful, giddie-eyed like Parrots, eaters
of others honours. (3.1.173)

Valentine is reduced to a stunned "You are angry." The Widow is
the equal of the witty intriguer and their equality of will, intellect,
and language leads to the paradoxical union of antagonists. There
is something of *The Tamer Tamed* here and even more of *Much Ado
about Nothing* and the verbal fencing of Beatrice and Benedick. In
Valentine and Lady Hartwell we can find prototypes, a bit coarser
to be sure, of the wild gallants and their witty ladies of Restoration
comedy.

The more sentimental figures of Lady Hartwell's sister, Isabel,
and Valentine's brother, Francisco, contrast with their voluble and
self-willed siblings. As characters neither is especially memorable,
but they add useful twists and turns to the plot and opportunities
for additional play of wit. Valentine is absolutely indifferent to the
financial straits in which his improvidence has placed his brother
and expects him to live by his wits as well: "*Frank,* stir, stir for
shame, thou art a pretty Scholar: ask how to live? write, write,
write any thing, the World's a fine believing World, write News"
(2.1.163). The tone is easy and relaxed; again the prose approaches
verse and the sense of the comic line is precise. There is an assured
laugh, not a little owing to the triplet of *writes* and the final two
beats, "write News," on the still freshly comic idea of writing
newsletters and pamphlets. That laugh is followed by another just
as certainly won in the next line by the faithful old servant, Lance:
"Dragons in *Sussex,* Sir, or fiery Battels seen in the Air at *Aspurge,*"
both topical references and generically apt to the sort of nonsense
that filled the newssheets.

Lady Hartlove is so horrified when she finds her sister sending
clothes and money to the attractive but impoverished Frank that
she orders her household to set out at once for the country. The
order provides an opportunity for extended country-city humor of
the sort later fully developed in the Restoration theater. Moreover,
she countermands the order immediately after her confrontation with
Valentine, providing dramatic punctuation to her romantic surrender.

Francisco is modest and shy. His good manners and elaborately courteous address to Isabel amusingly contrast with Valentine's slanging wars with the Widow. His shyness also supplies an excuse for getting him drunk enough to propose to Isabel. The last act is played in torchlight. Valentine is also drunk. Stage drunkenness may not be the most original of comic devices, but done well it serves its purpose. Fletcher writes his actors a thoroughly happy scene and the laughs are guaranteed.

Wit Without Money overturns one dramatic expectation after another but still concludes by satisfying the most basic expectation with the inevitable marriages. It does not flag in variety or richness of comic action, but its greatest strength is in the language. In scene after scene, characters, but especially Valentine, are given extended, witty arias. In Valentine and Lady Hartwell, moreover, Fletcher suggests a sexual equality that moves in the direction of a substantial social statement.

Monsieur Thomas (1610–16) is based in part on *L'Astrée* of Honoré d'Urfé, published in 1610. It may have been written as a play for the Children of the Queen's Revels.[5] Its date, however, is doubtful enough to allow it to be considered here. *Monsieur Thomas* shares with *Wit Without Money* come common character names, a last act in which many scenes take place in candlelit darkness, and, above all, a witty rakehell hero.

Monsieur Thomas is, however, rather more mixed in tone, for the plot is pure romance. Valentine has returned from his travels anxious to marry his beautiful ward, Cellide, who, despite their disparity in age, is ready to marry him. He has brought back with him an attractive young man, Francisco or Francis. When Francisco and Cellide fall in love, they both behave with the precious delicacy of manners associated with *L'Astrée*. Francisco, placing friendship above love, prepares to leave, and Cellide sacrifices her feelings to enter the local nunnery. The lovers are, of course, united in the fifth act when it is revealed that Francisco is Valentine's long-lost son, thus earning the play the alternate title of the 1639 quarto, *Father's Own Son.*

Samuel Taylor Coleridge declared a special fondness for this play: "I particularly recommend *Monsieur Thomas* for good pure comic humor."[6] No doubt he was thinking of the plot from which the title is taken. Thomas has also returned from his travels and faces a dilemma. Mary, Valentine's love and his intended bride, would have him behave with decorum, propriety, and even chastity. His father, Sebastian, on the other hand, wants a rakish, hell-raising, harum-scarum son, a Tom instead of a Monsieur Thomas.

The comedy is that of reversal and is worked to farcical extremes, but the farce is accompanied by Fletcher's sense of the comic line and of language that frequently transforms scenes of knockabout nonsense into genuine wit. Sebastian's shock at Tom's apparent transformation into a polite and polished gentleman is brilliantly caught: "Discretion? is it come to that? the boy's spoild" (*DW*, vol. 4; 1.2.434). His horror is compounded by the thought that Tom's travels have so refined him that he has taken to eating with a fork: "Undon without redemption: he eates with picks."

The two plots are loosely connected and different in tone, but each involves a father and a son and the precious gentility of Cellide and Francisco contrasts effectively with Tom's jolly coarseness. He too becomes *Father's Own Son* in one of the merriest scenes. Sebastian has become so despairing of Tom's ever recovering his proper masculine behavior that he decides he must remarry himself to beget a son more to his liking. But before he chooses a bride he interrogates Tom, "(For feare we confound our Genealogies)" (4.2.488), on his previous sexual activities with the maids and the neighboring wives and maidens. It turns out that Tom has slept with all the maids and with a wide selection of the neighboring women. Sebastian expresses his delight in a line that would be almost comfortable in a television sit-com: "The sisters of Saint *Albones,* all five; dat boy, / Dat's mine owne boy" (4.2.489).

A stage direction such as *"Madge with a divels vizard roring, offers to kisse him, and he fals down"* (3.3.478), on the other hand, shows Fletcher perfectly willing to indulge in even broader farce. Tom has been taunting the ladies with a fiddler. His fall comes as he climbs up to their balcony. The scene is accompanied with song, fiddling, and raucous noisemaking, recalling the bell-ringing in *The Little Thief.* The broadness of farcical action is matched by the language of the play's fat clown, Hylas, who boasts his attraction to all women, no matter their age or deformity:

> For those I love leade me to repentance:
> A woman with no nose, after my surquedry,
> Shewes like King *Philips* morall, *memento mori,*
> And she that has a wooden leg, demonstrates

> Like hypocrites, we halt before the gallowes:
> An old one with one tooth, seemes to say to us
> Sweet meats have sowre sauces: she's that's full of aches,
> Crum not your bread before you taste your porridge;
> And many morals may we finde.
>
> (4.4.493)

Hylas's speech works as a comic set piece. It has no real dramatic or thematic function; it is pure fun, as is the farce. The farce along with Hylas's antifeminism and the praise of ugly women reach back to their medieval roots. In the last act Fletcher treats the audience to a variation on the bed-trick. Thomas has disguised himself as his sister Dorothy (possibly one of the indications that *Monsieur Thomas* was originally written for the Boys); so disguised he has been able to trick Hylas into a mock marriage, gain access to the nunnery to extract Cellide, and finally to creep into (as he thinks) Mary's bed. The ladies, however, are in complete control of this skirmish in the war of the sexes. In the bed which has been pushed onto the stage a blackamoor has taken Mary's place. Dorothy and Mary observe and comment satirically as the randy Thomas approaches his comeuppance. "O, for gentle *Nicholas*" (5.5.502), cries Dorothy. This is not Chaucer's *Miller's Tale* and Tom will not be greeted with a hot colter, but his amazement when he discovers the black maid instead of Mary is Chaucerian: "Holy Saints, defend me. / The devill, devill, devill, devill, O the devill" (5.5.502).

Evoking the spirit of Chaucer is appropriate to *Monsieur Thomas*. The play is filled with fun and high jinks. The romantic plot is only partially integrated to the whole and functions largely as contrast in tone and language. The high spirits of the play, however, are never dampened. The marriages with which it ends are expected. Dorothy ends up with the silly Hylas, but symmetry here counts for more than reality. Mary's Thomas is untamed, but he will be married. The issues of the battle of the sexes are touched upon, but the spirit of comedy precludes their resolution. In *Monsieur Thomas* Fletcher demonstrates again his command of language and sense of the comic turn and produces a play which, for all its limitations, is eminently entertaining.

The Pilgrim (1621?) falls in Fletcher's later years although the date is uncertain. It belongs with those plays that draw on Spanish sources and influences, in this case Lope de Vega's *El Peregrino en*

Su Patria. It is, moreover, one of those plays that might almost be better classified as a tragicomedy since two characters are threatened, more or less seriously, with death. It is a romance interspersed with broadly comic scenes and with a star turn for the actor playing the irascible old father, Alphonso, who roars about the stage in search of his daughter, who has run off disguised as a boy to avoid being forced to marry the bandit chieftain and archenemy of her true love, who in turn has disguised himself as a pilgrim.

The Pilgrim has been called "one of Fletcher's happiest experiments in the comedy of Hispanic intrigue";[7] but, all in all, it is a fairly slapdash, albeit a frequently amusing, work. The extended scenes in a madhouse are not especially effective, although they must have appealed directly to the taste of the times, which found insanity a source of unending hilarity. Roderigo is a stock bandit figure who is actually a gentleman gone wrong through mistreatment, needing only a little kindness to lead him to reformation, but he manages a few minutes of almost genuine menace. Alphonso, the fierce old father, on the other hand, is a fine comic character with a wonderful bark:

> I say again, my horses,
> Are ye so hot? have ye your private Pilgrimages?
> Must ye be jumping, Joan? I'll wander with ye;
> I'll jump ye, and I'll juggle ye, my horses;
> And keep me this young Lirry-poop within doors,
> I will discover, Dame.
>   (*W*, vol. 5; 2.2.168)

Here is Fletcher's unmistakably English comic voice, bringing moments of life to an otherwise rather pale and artificial transplant. When *The Pilgrim* reaches beyond the ordinary constraints of the plot, it does so through Fletcher's command of a racy, colloquial comic idiom.

The Wild Goose Chase was played at court in the Christmas season of 1621/22 and was probably written in 1621. In the 1647 folio Humphrey Moseley wrote that *The Wild Goose Chase* "hath beene lost, and I feare irrecoverable; for a *Person of Quality* borrowed it from the *Actours* many years since, and (by the negligence of a Servant) it was never returned; therefore now I put up this *Si quis*, that whoever happily meetes with it, shall be thankfully satisfied if he please send it home" (Folio, A4). It was eventually sent home and published in folio in 1652, "one of the most handsome and elaborate issues of a single play in the times."[8]

The edition was printed for the benefit of John Lowin and Joseph Taylor, two leading actors of the King's Men during the reign of Charles I but by then no longer acting because of the closing of the theaters. In their dedicatory letter Lowin and Taylor, who originally played Belleur and Mirabel, describe its success and Fletcher's own pleased reaction: "The play was of so Generall a receiv'd Acceptance, that (he *Himself a Spectator*) we have known him unconcern'd, and to have wisht it had been none of His; He, as well as the *throng'd Theatre* (in despight of his innate Modesty, Applauding this *rare issue of his Brain*)" (*W*, vol. 4; 407).

Although *The Wild Goose Chase* was popular before the closing of the theaters, that popularity did not apparently extend to the Restoration. Samuel Pepys was anxious to see it because it was "a famous play." When he did, on 11 January 1667/68, he was disappointed, finding "nothing extraordinary at all, but very dull inventions and designs."[9] In a complimentary poem in the 1652 folio, on the other hand, Henry Harington praises the construction of the plot as pleasantly complex by which the audience is "glad to be deceiv'd, finding thy Drift / T' excell our guess at every turn, and shift" (*W*, vol. 4; 410). Nonetheless, *The Wild Goose Chase* was not among the most frequently revived Fletcher plays during the Restoration.

More recently it has been viewed as another one of Fletcher's precursors of the Restoration dramatic style and particularly of Congreve and the comedy of manners. This is a view corrected and qualified by Clifford Leech, who rightly points out Fletcher's remoteness from Congreve: "Fletcher strains towards the periphery of human experience, Congreve towards the centre."[10]

The Wild Goose Chase recalls *The Woman's Prize* and *Wit without Money* in its taming plot and *Monsieur Thomas* in making use of the motif of the returned travelers. Mirabel, the "Wild-goose," has been in no danger of being tamed by travel; instead his libertine inclinations have been reinforced:

> Give me the plump Venetian, fat, and lusty,
> That meets me soft and supple; smiles upon me,

As if a Cup of full Wine leapt to kiss me;
These slight things I affect not.

(1.2.320)

Among these "slight things" he numbers Oriana, De-Gard's sister, who not only loves him but is the girl his father hopes Mirabel
will marry. "Tye me to one smock? make my travels fruitless?"
(1.2.322). Mirabel's traveling companions, on the other hand, are
immediately caught by Nantolet's two daughters. Mirabel agrees
to coach his comrades, Belleur and Pinac, in their wooing. All three
girls are under the tutelage of Lugier, who coaches them in the
wiles and stratagems appropriate to the game of courtship.

The design of the play is loose, relying on incident and a pattern
of plot and counterplot and strained surprises rather than on careful
and complex construction. Oriana at last catches the Wild-goose,
but she herself is a disappointing, somewhat dim character. Nantolet's daughter, Rosalura and Lillia-Bianca, are by contrast lively
and spirited, suggestive of the equality of sexes essential to a true
comedy of manners. Belleur's condescending (and wittily put) bul-
lying, "Cry seriously, as if thou hadst lost thy Monkey" (4.2.368),
is sharply put down: "a man has manners; / A Gentleman, Civility,
and Breeding."

When the girls talk in private of men, however, their language
is far less mannered, suggestive instead of Jonson's Ladies Collegiate
in *Epicoene:*

Thou art a fool; give me a man brings Mettle,
Brings substance with him; needs no Broths to Lare him:
These little fellows shew like Fleas in boxes,
Hop up and down, and keep a stir to vex us;
Give me the puissant Pike, take you the small shot.

(3.1.349)

The equality here is a happily shared bawdy and Belleur's last words
at the end of the play, all the marriage pacts concluded, remind us
how far the play is from the comedy of manners: "No more for *Italy;*
for the *Low-Countries*" (5.6.390). *The Wild-goose Chase* perhaps gained
more reputation than it deserved through its separate publication
in folio, but Mirabel is an amusingly deplorable libertine, the chase
is lively and spirited, and Fletcher supplements his strong-willed,
witty rake with two witty, strong-willed females. The major strengths

of the play are in the vigorous language of its sexual flytings. Mirabel's libertinism almost meets a match in Lugier's enlightened view of morality and manners.

The last two comedies written solely by Fletcher, *The Chances* (1613–25) and *Rule a Wife and Have a Wife* (1624), are among his most popular plays. Both are comedies of Spanish intrigue, deriving their plots from Cervantes. *The Chances* is based on *La Señora Cornelia* from *Novelas Exemplares* published in 1613 and in a French translation in 1615.[11] It was revived often in the Restoration period; "The whole play pleases me well,"[12] wrote the often finicky Samuel Pepys. An "improved" version by George Villiers, the second duke of Buckingham, appeared in 1682, and the play was often acted and reprinted in the eighteenth and nineteenth centuries.

For all its popularity *The Chances* is a very slight comedy. At its best it exemplifies Fletcher's ability to transform a thin plot and stock characters into, at least on the testimony of its stage history, a more than passable entertainment. The plot is circumstantial, resting on a series of accidents and chances.

Two amorous young Spaniards, Don Frederick and Don John, have come to Bologna in search of a famed beauty. The beauty turns out to be Constantia, sister of Petruchio, the governor of Bologna, secretly betrothed to the Duke of Ferrara. The chance involvement of the Spaniards results in Don John being accidentally given Constantia's baby, his defending the Duke from assault by Petruchio, and Don Frederick taking Constantia to their boardinghouse under his protection. The conflict between Petruchio and the Duke is quickly resolved when the Duke reveals the secret betrothal and his intention to marry Constantia. The action is given a few more turns by the disappearance of Constantia and confusion of the Duke's Constantia with a runaway whore also named Constantia. The prologue, written for a revival of the play, correctly warns the audience not to "Expect strange turns, and windings in the Plot" but "sweet expression, quick conceit, / Familiar language" (*DW,* vol. 4; 628) and that is about what the play offers. The Duke and Constantia in character and language are of little interest; they belong to the traditional world of romance and tragicomedy. But the Spaniards— Don Frederick, the straight man, and Don John, the comedian— make an effective and amusing pair. Don John's bawdy rake role is also wittily set against Gillian (a fine Bolognaese name!), the sharp-tongued landlady, an epitome of bourgeois propriety.

John's lament, when he discovers the package he has been handed
is really a baby, is a sixty-eight-line tour de force of witty variations
on a theme of which a brief sample will serve to show its vigor:

> 'sdeath, have I
> Knowne Wenches thus long, all the wayes of wenches,
> Their snares and subtilties? have I read over
> All their Schoole learnings, div'd into their quiddits,
> And am I now bum-fidled with a Bastard!
>
> (1.5.558)

Gillian's language is equally forceful and spirited:

> Bring hither, as I say, to make my name
> Stinke in my neighbours nostrills, your Devises
> Your Brats, got out of *Alligant,* and broken oathes?
> Your Linsey Woolsey worke, your hasty puddings?
>
> (1.8.562)

This is the assured voice of a master of the comic idiom. *The Chances*
is filled with such language, the mark of Fletcher's dramatic genius
and key to his popular successes.

In 1773 the great actor-manager David Garrick published his
revision of Buckingham's alteration of *The Chances.* In his "Adver-
tisement" Garrick, assuming the play was by "Beaumont and
Fletcher," writes, "those authours, in this, as in many other of their
plays, seeming to grow tir'd of their subject, have finished it with
such unskilfulness and improbability which show at least, great
haste and negligence."[13] The last act, with its false conjuring (*"Two
shapes of women passe by"*; "Constantia *passes by"* [5.3.619]), and its
music and songs, both solemn and light, is a dramatic potpourri
that gives every indication of having been written with haste and
negligence, but with the haste and negligence of a deft and experienced professional who knows exactly how to please an audience.
Fletcher was not only not above the devices of what was to become
the music hall; he was a master of them.

Rule a Wife and Have a Wife (1624) was acted twice at court
within a few months of being licensed for the stage, suggesting that
its popularity was early established. It played throughout the Restoration and into the nineteenth century. One of its plots is derived

from Cervantes and the other less certainly from another Spanish source. The two gulling plots are deftly welded together and the whole play is well constructed.

Margarita, a rich heiress, plans to live the life of a female libertine and marries Leon, a timorous fool, in order to have her way. Instead of a fool, Leon turns out to be a trickster who, in the tradition of *The Taming of the Shrew*, brings her to heel and to a proper understanding of the duties of a wife: "Whither you will, I wait upon your pleasure; / Live in a hollow tree Sir, I'le live with ye" (*W*, vol. 3; 5.1.224). In a parallel cheating plot two skilled opponents reach a sort of cheaters' harmony. Estefania wants a husband and convinces the fortune-hunting Michael Perez that the house of her mistress, who is in fact Margarita, is her own. Perez marries her for the house, but passes himself off as worth marrying by giving her a casket of fake jewels as a dowry. Thus both cheaters are cheated. Estefania resolves all animosity by tricking the fat fool Cacafogo into giving her gold for the fake jewels.

The strengths of the play are in its tight dramatic construction, lively language, and satisfying use of the conventions of gulling comedy. Leon, Perez, and Estefania in particular are, moreover, choice comic roles. Leon has the delightful shift from a bumbling and shy fool to a forceful wife-tamer, and Estefania and Perez both happily gloat over their gulling triumphs and bemoan their defeats. *Rule a Wife and Have a Wife* is a happy and adroit comedy.

The Elder Brother (1625) is difficult to categorize as to author. The first performance was probably after Fletcher's death; and the play, originally by Fletcher, was most likely revised by Massinger. It is a frothy comedy that turns on the competition of two brothers, the elder an introverted scholar and the younger a foppish courtier. The elder is at first so indifferent to marriage that his father disinherits him; but when he meet Angelina, he changes his mind and enters into a sharp competition with his brother for the girl and for his inheritance. The story is filled out with rhapsodies in praise of learning, satire against courtiers, a little swordplay and heroics, and more bawdry.

Two remaining plays, *The Noble Gentleman* and *The Fair Maid of the Inn*, were licensed for the stage in 1626 after Fletcher's death. Both were attributed to Fletcher when they were licensed and are most certainly by him, but with the possibility of revision by others. The main plot of *The Noble Gentleman*, the elaborate duping of

Monsieur Marine into believing he has been created a duke and his
treatment at the hands of his wife and two sharpers, involves both
the matters of gulling and husband taming, and Monsieur Marine
is one of Fletcher's pleasingly eccentric fools. The play also uses the
country-city dichotomy that was to form a staple conflict on the
Restoration stage where it continued to be acted. Unlike *The Noble
Gentleman, The Fair Maid of the Inn* was not a popular play. It well
may have been Fletcher's last play, written alone and then revised
by others, but it may still best be passed over in silence.

Fletcher in Collaboration

Three of the plays classified as collaborative and included in the
1647 folio are of such uncertain history and attribution that they
may be dismissed from consideration. *Love's Cure, or The Martial
Maid* (1605?–25?) may have been written for the children early in
the collaboration of Beaumont and Fletcher and later revised extensively by Philip Massinger. "Nearly everything about the play,"
G. E. Bentley concludes, "is in a state of confusion."[14] The gulling
comedy *Wit At Several Weapons* (1609–20) also has a confused history
of authorship and production. The current consensus of opinion
gives the play entirely to Thomas Middleton and William Rowley.
Finally, *The Nice Valour, or The Passionate Madman* (ca. 1615–25),
with its antiduelling satire and the absurd coward Lapet, who has
written a book called "The Uprising of the *Kick;* / And the downfall
of the *Duello*" (*W,* vol. 10; 4:184), the shortest of the plays in the
folio, is thought to be predominantly the work of Thomas Middleton.

Six collaborative comedies remain to be considered. *The Beggars'
Bush* is the work of Beaumont, Fletcher, and Massinger. Four plays
represent solely the Fletcher-Massinger collaboration: *The Little French
Lawyer, The Custom of the Country, The Sea Voyage,* and *The Spanish
Curate.* In *The Maid in the Mill* Fletcher collaborated with William
Rowley, the playwright-actor who specialized in fat clown roles.

Coleridge's enthusiastic view of *Beggars' Bush* (ca. 1612–22) nicely
catches the spirit of the play: "In romantic drama, Beaumont and
Fletcher are almost supreme. Their plays are in general most truly
delightful. I could read the Beggar's Bush [*sic*] from morning to
night. How sylvan and sunshiny it is!"[15] Its displaced duke disguised
as a merchant and his loyal subjects (under his father as their "King")
masquerading in the midst of a gang of jolly beggars, roistering in

the tavern, and wandering in the wood, recall Shakespeare's Forest of Arden, the roguery in *The Winter's Tale,* and the flavor of Thomas Dekker's comic world. In spite of its tragicomic overtones, *Beggars' Bush* is not really all that serious. In it nothing is dull.

The usurping Duke, Woolfort, is roundly excoriated by the loyal Hubert as "A Prince, in nothing but your beastly lusts, / And boundless rapines" (*DW,* vol. 3; 1.2.252). Although the plot is filled with all the twists and turns, plots and counterplots of tragicomedy, the overall feeling of the play is romantic and pastoral, indeed, "sylvan and sunshiny." Woolfort is utterly unrepentant at the end, remaining the tragicomic villian: "Who, I repent? / And say I'm sorry? yes, 'tis a fooles language / And not for *Woolfort"* (5.2.328). But the audience is finally left with the more cheerful lack of repentance on the part of the beggars who, rather than accepting a reformed life in Flanders, decide to transfer their quasi-larcenous activities to England.

The portions of the play attributed to Fletcher, acts 3 and 4, contain some of the liveliest and most entertaining scenes. Act 3 is set in a tavern where the beggars play their cheating tricks. At the sound of a "Sowgelders horn" Higgen, dressed in the garb of that trade, enters, accompanied by a piper, and sings *"Have ye any worke for the Sow-gelder, hoa."* This song is followed by two more in the same spirit and by a juggling act while the customers in the tavern have their pockets picked. The father of the true duke (the ducal line in this case flows through the late duchess) now enters *"like a blinde Aquavitae-man, and a boy singing the Song."* This music-hall turn is neatly integrated with the romantic and tragicomic plot lines.

Fletcher also entertains the audience with his command of rogues' canting language:

> I crowne thy nab, with a gage of benbouse,
> And stall thee by the salmon into the clowes,
> To mand o' the pad, and strike all the cheates;
> To mill from the Ruffmans, commission and slates,
> Twang dell's i' the stromell, and let the Quire Cuffin:
> And Herman Becks trine, and trine to the Ruffin.
>   (3.4.294–95)

Even if this is truly rendered, rhyming back slang of the London underworld rather than the Flanders where the play is set, the world evoked by *Beggars's Bush* is also that of Breughel and Dutch genre painting.

The Little French Lawyer (1619–23), written in collaboration with Philip Massinger, was also a favorite of Coleridge. If taken as a serious comic statement, the play, in its main plot at least, is an appallingly brutal piece of masculine ferocity in which two young women are nearly frightened out of their wits with threats of rape and murder, one because she has married an older man and has rejected her former wooer's adulterous advances, the second because in a variation on the popular stage bed-trick she lay still and did not reveal herself not to be the old man with whom the young rake thought he was sharing the bed.

The Little French Lawyer is not high comedy, and it finally does not reach beyond varied entertainment with each scene to be taken for its own sake. The subplot, from which the play derives its title, does have a thesis in its antidueling matter. Dinant is furious that his love Lamira has, at her father's demand, married the rich old sailor, probably a pirate, named Champernell. He challenges Champernell to a duel which is answered—Champernell being too old and battered from the wars—by his nephew and Lamira's brother.

When Lamira hears of the proposed duel, she sends Dinant to the other side of town on a fool's errand so that his life will not be risked. Cleremont, Dinant's friend and second, thus is left to face two opponents when he arrives at the dueling field. He asks passersby to stand with him, but the first is an old man who wears no sword; next, two gentlemen decline because they are on their way to a duel themselves; finally La-Writ, the Little Lawyer with his bag of briefs, agrees to fight in Dinant's place. "Help me to pluck my Sword out then, quickly, quickly, / "Thas not seen Sun these ten years" (*W*, vol. 3; 2.1.395)

The little lawyer, as one expects in the comic world, turns out to be a skilled duelist who quickly disarms his opponents and sends them home in defeat. La-writ is now metamorphosized into a fiery duelist who returns to normal only after he has sent a challenge to the President of the Court and through Cleremont's tricks been left shivering in his shirt on the dueling field. La-writ's comedy is of the worm-turned, playing on size and expectations of behavior rather than on any verbal wit; but he provides some effective scenes, and his advice after his reform is sound enough:

> Drink Wine, and eat good meat, and live discreetly,
> Talk little, 'tis an antidote against a beating;
> Keep thy hand from thy sword, and from thy Laundress placket,
> And thou wilt live long.
>
> (5.1.450)

Dinant and Cleremont, the two wits, are less charming and far less steadily seen. The elaborate deceit they practice on the two women, staging a mock capture by bandits, threatening them with rape, murder, and the execution of their friends, is almost Websterian in its potential sadism. "A Horrid noise of Musique within, *Enter one and opens the door, in which* Lamira *and* Anabel *were shut, they in all fear*" (5.1.440), reads the stage direction at the start of act 5. The strange sounds evoke a moment of poetry as Anabel ascribes them to "The wind I think, murmuring amongst old rooms" (5.1.440).

Still what with the thieves "peeping" here and there and Anabel's sturdy defiance, "Pox peep 'em," and her sudden and surely unwarranted decision that

> This is a punishment, upon our own prides
> Most justly laid; we must abuse brave Gentlemen,
> Make 'em tame fools, and hobby-horses, laugh and jear at
> Such men too, and so handsom and so Noble,
> That howsoe're we seem'd to carry it—
> Wou'd 'twere to do again. . . .
>
> (5.1.440)

none of the threats can be taken seriously. The tragicomic edge to *The Little French Lawyer* is parodic. The thieves are not thieves but gentlemen masqueraders, and the rakehell wits turn out not to be the libertines they seemed. Cleremont happily marries Anabel and Dinant is content with Champernell's offer of "Another Neice, to this not much inferiour" (5.1.453), a true comic vision of a world filled with infinitely replaceable and marriageable nieces.

The Little French Lawyer's popularity is understandable. It has a bit of everything in it: farcical comedy and bawdry, melodrama, and sentiment. Although the characters are not fully realized and frequently inconsistent, they are interesting for their embryonic potential in the later development of the stage. Lamira waffles in her attitude toward Dinant, but she is primarily concerned with making certain that Champernell and Dinant both recognize her independence and respect, not simply her honor, but her own intentions to guard that honor and her basic integrity as a woman. Dinant and Cleremont are not Jonsonian Truewits, but they suggest the potential of Truewit as the character will be shaped in the Restoration. Finally, however, when the audience, pleased and laughing, leaves the theater, the conversations will not be about ideas or character, but action and spectacle, the thieves' cave, the music, and the once ferocious little lawyer shivering in his shirt.

   The Custom of the Country is another Fletcher and Massinger collaboration that achieved considerable popularity and, indeed, notoriety. Richard Lovelace lists *The Custom of the Country* in the margin of his commendatory poem in the Beaumont and Fletcher folio when he praises Fletcher for his proper language:

> *View here a loose thought said with such a grace,*
> Minerva *might have spoke in* Venus *face;*
> *So well disguis'd, that t'was conceiv'd by none*
> *But* Cupid *had* Diana's *linnen on.* . . .
>   *(Folio, b3)*

John Dryden thought otherwise, and when defending Restoration comedy against charges of lewdness in his preface to *Fables Ancient and Modern* (1700), he wrote that "There is more Bawdry in one play of Fletcher's call'd *The Custom of the Country,* than in all ours together."[16]

   When Samuel Pepys saw it in January 1667/68 he too was not pleased, finding it "fully the worst play that ever I saw or I believe shall see." Pepys's opinion does not seem to reflect popular taste. An early indication of *The Custom of the Country*'s success is that its revival in November 1628 earned Sir Henry Herbert, Charles I's master of the revels, over seventeen pounds as his share of receipts in a benefit performance, the largest amount he lists earned from a group of plays that included *Othello, Richard II,* and *The Alchemist.* Its revival in London in 1983 in an adaptation by Nicholas Wright does not argue for contemporary popularity, but at least that there is life in the old play yet.

   The Custom of the Country is a skillful and unabashedly deliberate mixture of tragicomic romance and farcical comic bawdry in the guise of a chastity play. In the end chastity and marriage triumph over lechery and lust, but the audience meanwhile has been entertained with the lubricity of Count Clodio threatening the heroine with the exercise of the custom of the country, the *droit du seigneur*, the right of the ruler to the first night with a bride after her marriage; with the hero sexually pursued by a beautiful man-eating female; and with the sight of the aptly named Rutilio, brother of the hero, happily and then unhappily rutting away, until he loses his taste for lechery, as the chief worker in a male bawdy house.

The main plot is thoroughly romantic. Arnoldo and his bride, Zenochia, accompanied by the randy Rutilio, flee from Clodio's intended execution of the custom of the country on the chaste Zenochia. Their ship is taken by Leopold. Although Arnoldo and Rutilio manage to escape capture by swimming ashore, Zenochia is taken and given by Leopold to the lady he loves but who does not return his love, Hippolyta.

Events become increasingly complex when Hippolyta falls in love with Arnoldo and attempts to seduce him, even threatening him with rape, only to encounter his stern virtue and unshakeable loyalty to Zenochia. Rutilio now becomes embroiled in a duel with the conceited duelist, Duarte. He apparently kills him, but is given sanctuary from the police by Duarte's mother, Guiomar, who is unaware that her son is involved until his body is brought in. Even then the noble lady keeps her word and does not betray Rutilio to the police. Another mishap, however, results in his arrest as a suspicious character. He is saved from the police by the bawd Sulpitia, who recognizes his potential for her male bordello and immediately sets him to work.

Meanwhile, Hippolyta, thoroughly bad, threatens to have Zenochia strangled unless Arnoldo satisfies her lust. Zenochia, preferring death to Arnoldo's dishonor, urges him not to yield. The arrival of the Governor and Count Clodio, now a completely reformed character because of the dangers of his sea voyage, saves Zenochia, but a few more twists and turns remain before virtue and marriage may triumph.

Hippolyta has been checked but not foiled. Now she has Sulpitia prepare a magic charm against Zenochia and the poor girl begins to waste away. Duarte, the conceited young man apparently killed by Rutilio, recovers; not only does he regain his health, but as a consequence of the salutary bleeding given him, he regains his fundamental sense of decency and honor. He now considers Rutilio his spiritual savior and seeks him out in the bawdy house, rescuing him not just from a fate worse than death, but from probable death from sexual exhaustion and disease.

Rutilio is so enervated and his lusts so cooled by his labors in the bordello that he decides to marry. Duarte's mother, Guiomar, seems to him the most likely candidate. One more peak and turn of action comes when Duarte, who disguised, has not told his mother he is alive, carries Rutilio's letter of proposal to Guiomar. Duarte is disgusted at the idea that his mother might marry his supposed murderer and carries the letter as a test of her and of womankind. Guiomar is equally outraged that Rutilio would have the audacity to think she would marry the man who killed her son. So she pretends to welcome the proposal and prepares a trap for Rutilio. When he arrives to claim her as a bride, her servants seize him and she demands justice from the Governor. The only justice available is his death. Guiomar is reluctant to demand this. The dilemma is resolved when Duarte reveals himself and Guiomar agrees to marry the apologetic and reformed Rutilio.

As Zenochia grows weaker and weaker, Arnoldo himself begins to fade away. Hippolyta is so moved by this that she undergoes a swift reformation and calls in Sulpitia to remove the malignant charm. The various Jacks and Jills are assigned to their appropriate partners and the audience leaves Blackfriars happily assured by Arnoldo of the morality of the spectacle they have witnessed:

> . . . the unspotted progress of our loves
> Ends not alone in safety, but reward,
> To instruct others, by our fair example;
> That though good purposes are long withstood,
> The hand of Heaven still guides such as are good.
> (W, vol. 1; 5.1.386)

Fletcher and Massinger make skillful use of their apparent sources and *The Custom of the Country* is tightly plotted; the comic, romantic, and tragicomic materials easily integrated. Zenochia and Arnoldo are straightforward romantic protagonists given to noble and heroic speeches. Each functions as a defender of chastity, and there is a nice balance in the threats Zenochia undergoes from Clodio and Arnoldo's similar situation at the hands of Hippolyta. The latter case, however, is qualified by an undertone of comedy and by the parodic, parallel adventures of Rutilio.

Arnoldo's situation is a perversion of the traditional romance pattern in which the stranger hero is instantly beloved of the romantic heroine and wins a lovely bride. Hippolyta, one of Fletcher's wicked lecherous females, comically reverses the romantic myth. She is the lecher's mythic dream but the anathema of the romantic lover such as Arnoldo. Arnoldo's chaste rejection of Hippolyta's friendly offers is essential and legitimate in the world of romance, but quite something else in the realm of Saturnalian comedy.

Rutilio's consignment to the male stews is another comic dream come true and Fletcher's language soars:

> This old Cat will suck shrewdly; you have no daughters?
> I flye at all: now am I in my Kingdom.
> Tug at an Oar? no, tug in a Feather-bed,
> I'le make you young again, believe that Lady.
> I will so frubbish you.
>
> (3.3.343)

But the dream turns into a bizarre, outrageous, and uproarious nightmare, a sure cure for lechery:

> More women yet?
> Would I were honestly married
> To any thing that had but half a face,
> And not a groat to keep her, nor a smock,
> That I might be civilly merry when I pleased,
> Rather than labouring in these Fulling-mills.
>
> (4.1.365)

Rutilio and his dream gone wrong are Fletcher's creation and the source of most of the comic life of *The Custom of the Country*. Rutilio is an endearing grotesque, an excellent stage role, and a witty commentary on sexual aspirations and realities.

For all its inane plot, or perhaps because of it, *The Custom of the Country* is, while not great comedy, effective comedy. Fletcher and Massinger's collaboration is polished and finished, almost without seams. The blend of tone and action, of romance, tragicomedy, and broad comedy gives the play considerable variety, but finally also enhances the comic spirit of the whole endeavor. This placketchasing world and its foibles are not to be taken seriously no matter in what voice it speaks. Whatever its drawbacks, moreover, *The Custom of the Country* is the work of two playwrights who knew what their audience wanted and gave it to them with professional agility.

The Sea Voyage (1622) is a rough and ready variation of *The Tempest,* but it is Shakespearean only at a great distance. The opening storm scene echoes the storm in *The Tempest* and there are numerous other parallels of character and incident, but in spite of a few sententious passages in praise of virtue in the abstract, Fletcher and Massinger are only interested in producing a fast-paced show that easily shifts from romance to bawdry and back again without a hint of any larger comic or typological significance.

Whether Fletcher revised a Massinger-Fletcher collaboration or Massinger revised a Fletcher original is still in debate, but the major comic scenes are not far from the bordello humor of *The Custom of the Country*. They also revert to Fletcher's hungry comedy—this time with a fillip of cannibalism combined with sex. The rogues threaten to turn the romantic heroine into supper when they are interrupted by the timely arrival of the comic lead, Tibalt. A bit of the scene is worth quoting because it nicely illustrates Fletcher's command of the comic idiom.

Lamure.	Mary wee'll eat your Ladiship.
Franville.	You that have buried us in this base Island,
	Wee'll bury ye in a more noble Monument.
Surgeon.	Will ye say your prayers, that I may perform Lady?
	We are wondrous sharp set; come Gentlemen,
	Who are for hinder parts.
Morillat.	I.
Franville.	I.
Lamure.	And I.
Surgeon.	Be patient;
	They will not fall to every Man's share.
Aminta.	O hear me;
	Hear me ye barbarous men.
Morillat.	Be short and pithy,
	Our stomachs cannot stay a long discourse.
Surgeon.	And be not fearful,
	For I'll kill ye daintily.

Aminta.	Are ye not *Christians*?
Lamure.	Why, do not *Christians* eat Women?
	[*Enter* Tibalt, Master, Saylors.]
Aminta.	Eat one another? 'tis more impious.
Surgeon.	Come, come.
Aminta.	Oh, help, help, help.
Tibalt.	The Ladies voice! stand off slaves,
	What do you intend villains?
	I have strength enough left me, if you abuse this soul,
	To—
Master.	They would have ravisht her upon my life,
	Speak, how was it Lady?
Aminta.	Forgive 'em, 'twas their hungers.
Tibalt.	Ha, their hungers!
Master.	They would have eaten her.
Tibalt.	O dam'd villains; speak Is it true?
Surgeon.	I confess an appetite.
Tibalt.	An appetite, I'll fit ye for an appetite.
	Are ye so sharp set, that her flesh must serve you?
	Murther's a main good service with your Worships;
	Since you would be such Devils,
	Why did you not begin with one another handsomly,
	And spare the Woman to beget more food on?

$$\text{(}W\text{, vol. 9; 3.1.31–32)}$$

The extended quotation shows that Fletcher not only does not let go of the joke; he keeps building on it to a witty climax. Cannibalism is always, under the right conditions, good for a laugh, and even more so when it involves an especially attractive snack. Aminta adds to the joke by playing the straight woman—not simply the lady in extreme distress, but the heroine who never drops her role of unending forgiveness. The whole joke is inevitably capped by Tibalt's witty sexual turn. This is not high comedy, but it is skilled gag writing. It would be a dull and stuffy audience that failed to appreciate this sort of comic skill. *The Sea Voyage* is a poor play if one compares it to *The Tempest*, but lively and outrageous fun if accepted on its own terms.

The last two collaborations of Fletcher and Massinger in comedy show the same command of comic technique and unpretentious aims. Both plays are the work of men at ease in cooperative composition and in total command of their theatrical milieu. *The Spanish Curate,* licensed and acted in 1622, draws on Spanish sources and is a mix of tragicomedy intrigue and cuckold comedy tied to the comic business of the Spanish curate, Lopez, and Diego, his sexton. By and large Massinger handles the tragicomic portions while Fletcher writes the laughing comedy. It is not a memorable play, but shows able carpentry in tacking together rather thin stuff to create, if not a very good play, a collection of workable scenes.

Lopez and Diego are good comic roles and Fletcher writes them some genuinely amusing scenes. When they threaten to leave their congregation because of its shocking dormancy in weddings, births, and deaths and consequent loss of fees, Fletcher's command of fresh, specific, detailed and totally convincing idiomatic comic language is again evident:

> *Lopez.* Let Weddings, Christnings, Churchings, Funerals,
> And merry Gossipings go round, go round still,
> Round as a Pig, that we may find the profit.
>
> *Diego.* And let your old men fall sick handsomely,
> And dye immediately, their Sons may shoot up:
> Let Women dye o'th' Sullens too, 'tis natural,
> But be sure their Daughters be of age first,
> That they may stock us still: your queazie young Wives
> That perish undeliver'd, I am vext with,
> And vext abundantly, it much concerns me,
> There's a Child's Burial lost, look that be mended.
>   (*W,* vol. 2; 3.2.94)

This is a rich and genuine comic voice. Its satire is absolutely good natured, accepting of human foibles, broadly generous; Lopez's jibes at the Puritans are no surprise:

> 'Tis wel, proceed Neighbours,
> I am glad I have brought ye to understand good manners,
> Ye had Puritan hearts a-while, spurn'd at all pastimes,
> But I see some hope now.

And there is hope in the song that parishioners now sing, "Let the Bells ring, and let the Boys sing" (3.2.95). One advantage surely of collaborative writing was that the playwright was essentially concerned with scenes, and at scenes Fletcher was a master.

The final comic collaboration to be mentioned, *The Maid in the Mill* (1623), was written with the fat actor William Rowley, who wrote into the play a substantial clown's role ideally suited to his own talent. Three performances before the court attest to its early popularity. It is a slight and fluffy bit of nonsense with the familiar mixture of romance, moments of tragicomic melodrama, and a good dose of bawdy. Fletcher's main contribution is a lively scene in which one of the romantic heroines, a miller's daughter who in fact turns out to be the daughter of a nobleman, having been abducted and threatened with rape if she does not yield to her abductor, cools his lust by pretending to be an outright wanton.

The Count is deeply shocked by the virtuous Florimell's whorish behavior and language:

> Otrante.   Are ye no Maid?
>
> Florimell.   Alas (my Lord) no certain:
> I am sorry you are so innocent to think so,
> Is this an age for silly Maids to thrive in?
> It is so long too since I lost it Sir,
> That I have no belief I ever was one:
> What should you do with Maiden-heads? you hate 'em,
> They are peevish, pett[ish] things, that hold no game up,
> No pleasure neither, they are sport for Surgeons:
> I'll warrant you I'll fit you beyond Maiden-head:
> A fair and easie way men travel right in,
> And with delight, discourse, and twenty pleasures,
> They enjoy their journey; mad men creep through hedges.
> (W, vol 7; 5.2.63)

Florimell's language shows she was raised in a mill, and there is little reason for Otrante not to be shocked. Five improper songs add to his dismay and the overall rowdy fun of the scene:

> *Think me still in my Fathers Mill,*
> *where I have oft been found-a*
> *Thrown on my back, on a well-fill'd sack,*
> *while the Mill has still gone round-a:*

> *Prethe sirah try thy skill,*
> *and again let the Mill go round-a.*
>   (5.2.63)

Here are those loose thoughts said with grace that Richard Lovelace admired. Fletcher writes a thoroughly bawdy scene, but the bawdry is all in the cause of virtue. This is having a bawdy cake and eating it too.

Fletcher's comic world is varied in tone, in dramatic types, in characters, and in the range of comic language. Romance and tragicomedy mix easily with comedy of wit, satire, farce, and bawdy horseplay. Grotesques leer out from dark corners and varieties of clowns dance and cavort in sunny meadows and beery taverns. The range and strength of his comic language is remarkable and extends far beyond the witty exchange of gentlemen on their way to the comedy of manners of the Restoration. If there is not a coherent comic vision, there is a sure sense of human folly and absurdity; and there is a plentitude of surprise and laughter, a superb sense of comic timing, of the structures of action and language that make up the comic moment.

Chapter Six
"Fletcher's *Flourishing Bayes*": Reputation and Achievement

Reputation

Fletcher's bays have inevitably faded over the years, but he remains an important figure in the history and development of the English stage. It would be depressing indeed if one could write today, as John Dryden did in *An Essay of Dramatic Poesy* in 1668, that "Their [Beaumont and Fletcher's] plays are now the most pleasant and frequent entertainments of the stage; two of theirs being acted through the year for one of Shakespeare's or Jonson's: the reason is, because there is a certain gaiety in their comedies, and pathos in the more serious plays, which suit generally with all men's humours. Shakespeare's language is likewise a little obsolete and Ben Jonson's wit comes short of theirs."[1] Happily Shakespeare and Jonson have been restored to their proper estimation after their temporary displacement or underestimation in the later seventeenth century.

The criticism of the seventeenth century repeated a set of comparative platitudes about Shakespeare, Jonson, and Fletcher. Richard Flecknoe, writing in *A Discourse of the English Stage* in 1664, presents the standard view, frequently repeated throughout the rest of the century, that "Shakespeare excelled in a natural vein, Fletcher in wit and Jonson in gravity and ponderousness of style; whose only fault was that he was too elaborate and had he mixed less erudition with his plays, they had been more pleasant and delightful than they are. Comparing him with Shakespeare, you shall see the difference nature and art; and with Fletcher the difference between wit and judgement."[2] Fletcher was also regularly praised for the ease of his dialogue and for his inventiveness.

More than critical lip service, however, was paid to the works of Fletcher and Beaumont on the Restoration stage; revivals of their plays provided a major staple for the London stages, a direct link with the Jacobean stage and its values, and a model for the emerging playwrights of the Restoration. Moreover, the publication of the second folio, *Fifty Comedies and Tragedies,* in 1679, indicated the continuing interest in the plays both for theatergoers and for readers. The second folio included all the plays in the first folio and eighteen plays hitherto uncollected. For the Restoration Fletcher and Beaumont were still vital, living playwrights, not historical monuments.

Three editions of the works of Beaumont and Fletcher were published in the eighteenth century: in 1711, 1750, and 1778. However, when George Coleman the Elder wrote in the preface to his 1778 edition, a defensive, if not to say huckstering, note was already evident: "For our parts we have been incited to this undertaking from a real admiration of these poets, grounded, as we apprehended, on their genuine excellencies, and a thorough persuasion that the works of Beaumont and Fletcher may proudly claim a second place in the English drama, nearer to the first than to the third, to those of Shakespeare; some of their plays being so much in his manner, that they can scarcely be distinguished to be the work of another hand."[3] Fletcher and his inevitably linked collaborator were well on the way to becoming not merely antiquities, but antiquities of somewhat doubtful propriety.

Neoclassical criticism, heightened concern for propriety and morality on the stage, and the growing recognition of Shakespeare's genius, despite his "irregularities," all took their toll on the reputation of Fletcher and Beaumont, who were increasingly relegated to a less and less august position in the dramatic hierarchy. Throughout the eighteenth century the tragedies and tragicomedies steadily disappeared from the repertoire and the comedies competed with less and less success against Shakespeare's late romances. In the mid-century *Rule a Wife and Have a Wife* was performed fifty times in seventeen seasons, but as Lawrence B. Wallis has observed, "this was only a mediocre stockplay achievement."[4] George Coleman the Elder successfully revived *Philaster* in 1763 at Drury Lane; his version ran for seventeen performances and established William Powell as a star. The recent failures of such hitherto popular revivals as *The Little French Lawyer, The Spanish Curate,* and *The Scornful Lady,* however, convinced Coleman that *Philaster* needed drastic revision to appeal to the tastes of the day. He modified whatever he considered ribald and obscene, cut the play by a third, and removed the wounding of Arethusa and Bellario by Philaster.[5]

Throughout the eighteenth century playwrights continued to use

Fletcher and Beaumont as a sort of dramatic mine, lifting and adapting scenes, themes, and sometimes whole plays, but the overall decline in popularity was inexorable. In the nineteenth century three editions of the complete plays of Beaumont and Fletcher appeared: Henry Weber's in 1812; George Darley's in 1840; and what was to be the scholarly edition for the next sixty years, that of the Reverend Alexander Dyce in 1843–46. Dyce's edition was republished in Boston and New York in 1854 and Darley's edition was republished in 1866.

These editions may be seen as relating to a general decline in interest in Elizabethan and Jacobean plays as plays to be acted on the stage and an increasing interest in the drama of the past as literature. Changes in the theaters themselves—the shift to the proscenium-arch stage, the introduction of elaborate scenery, the growth in the size of the auditorium—all contributed to the conditions that made Shakespeare seem unactable to a critic like Charles Lamb. Lamb, however, contributed to a literary interest in Fletcher by including Fletcher and Beaumont in his *Specimens of English Dramatic Poets* (1808), a work that served to keep alive at least a reading interest in the old dramatists.

Samuel Taylor Coleridge read the plays and commented on them extensively. Most of his commentary is negative. He objects to their politics and their morality. Beaumont and Fletcher are "high-flying passive obedience Tories" whose plays are filled with "the minutiae of a lecher" and who "always write as if Virtue or Goodness were a sort of Talisman or Strange Something that might be lost without the least fault on the part of the Owner."[6] Coleridge, moreover, always looked at Fletcher in relation to Shakespeare, a point of view inevitably disadvantageous to Fletcher. Nonetheless, he also wrote that "Beaumont and Fletcher are the most lyrical of our dramatists" and "In the romantic drama, Beaumont and Fletcher are almost supreme. Their plays are in general most truly delightful. . . . How lamentable it is that no gentlemen and scholar can be found to edit these beautiful plays! Did the name of criticism ever descend so low as in the hands of those two fools and knaves, Seward and Simpson?"[7] The passionate snarl at the editors of the 1750 edition is not solely the consequence of respect for Fletcher, but Coleridge's views certainly have the weight of passionate attention.

Although the plays virtually disappeared from the stage in the nineteenth century, critical interest was kept alive. Fletcher suffered

from comparison with Shakespeare and from charges of immorality,
but a core of respect and admiration remained, in particular for his
lyricism. At the end of the century Algernon Charles Swinburne
was writing in rather heated prose that Fletcher's

> crown of praise is to have created a wholly new and wholly delightful form
> of mixed comedy or dramatic romance, dealing merely with the humours
> and sentiments of men, their passions and their chances; to have woven
> of all these a web of emotion and event with such gay dexterity, to have
> blended his colours and combined his effects with such exquisite facility
> and swift light sureness of touch, that we may return once again from
> those heights and depths of poetry to which access was forbidden him,
> ready as ever to enjoy as of old the fresh incomparable charm, the force
> and ease and grace of life, which fill and animate the radiant world of his
> romantic imagination.[8]

For Swinburne, at least, Fletcher's withered bays were greening,
and he was seen as having something like his old stature.

In the early twentieth century increasing scholarly interest in
Elizabethan and Jacobean theater brought about the start of an
ambitious but finally incomplete Variorum Edition of *The Works of
Francis Beaumont and John Fletcher*. Four volumes were completed
from 1905 to 1912 under the general editorship of A. H. Bullen.
The Glover and Waller edition of *The Works* in ten volumes appeared
in 1905–12.

Study of stage conditions and the increasing scholarly interest in
the dramatic texts of the past resulted in a more balanced view of
Fletcher. G. C. Macaulay tempered his praise with qualifications
over Fletcher's morality, but recognized his stagecraft: "The impres-
sion made upon the mind of the reader of this large collection of
plays is one of astonishment at the richness and variety of dramatic
invention which they display; but it is seldom that he is able to
commend one of these dramas without very serious reservations,
either moral or artistic. The merit belongs usually to particular
scenes in a drama rather than to the drama as a whole; and in cases
where there is no ground for criticizing the conduct of the design,
it is often found that the plot deals with morbid or doubtful
situations."[9]

In his commendatory poem in the 1649 folio the playwright
Richard Brome had written, *"His* Scenes *were* Acts, *every* Act *a* Play"
(Folio, g). By restriking this note Macaulay affirms one of the major

critical recognitions of Fletcher's dramatic skill, his ability to craft individual scenes. The objections he raises continue to be raised, although the charges of immorality have become somewhat muted.

Whether the Cambridge University Press edition of *The Dramatic Works of the Beaumont and Fletcher Canon* under the general editorship of Fredson Bowers is an indication more of an increase in Fletcher's reputation than of the thoroughness and industry of contemporary textual studies is perhaps open to question, but the edition will be a distinguished monument to Fletcher when completed. The growing amount of criticism written concerning Fletcher is another mark of his enduring and possibly growing importance within the Jacobean dramatic canon.

Tucker Brooke's summation of Fletcher's merits in *A Literary History of England* may stand as a fairly typical mid-century assessment: "The reading of Fletcher is like a long voyage through a tropical archipelago. The air is sultry and tempestuous, the landscapes are over-florid; but no one forgets the experience, though most of the details—except the magnificent songs and the electric scenes of tension—will soon fade from memory."[10] The deflation of the reputation over the years is complete, but sympathetic readers still find pleasure and value in reading Fletcher.

Robert Ornstein may be taken as exemplifying a more irritated and impatient view of Fletcher, one tending to reduce the size of his reputation. He finds the "ethical frivolity of Fletcher's drama" "thoroughly premeditated and in fact the work of a highly skilled and disciplined craftsman" and consequently "disturbing and reprehensible. . . ."[11] But the book-length studies of Fletcher by Eugene Waith, William Appleton, Clifford Leech, and Nancy Cotton Pearse show, as well as do numerous journal articles, that Fletcher's reputation has survived sufficiently to keep him a subject of scholarly interest.

Unfortunately, one cannot say as much for his actual theatrical reputation, at least not on the basis of productions in the twentieth century. *The Faithful Shepherdess* received two productions, but it is hardly a name to conjure by. The one play in the Beaumont and Fletcher canon that is consistently acted year after year, by both amateurs and professionals, is *The Knight of the Burning Pestle*, attributed entirely to Francis Beaumont.

Since 1975 *The Maid's Tragedy* and *The Custom of the Country* have both been acted; the rest is silence. Obviously many more are worth revival—*Monsieur Thomas* and *The Humorous Lieutenant* come immediately to mind. John Fletcher will never again be seriously compared with Ben Jonson or William Shakespeare, but his reputation is undoubtedly more secure than it was in the nineteenth century, and if dramatic exploration of the Jacobean stage continues, Fletcher's plays will find audiences.

Praise and Otherwise: The Achievement

No small part of Fletcher's achievement is his influence on the Restoration theater and the extension of his popularity well beyond the times and milieu in which his plays had originally flourished. If his contributions, including his role in the development of tragicomedy, were not strictly innovative, but a part of a changing theatrical milieu, nonetheless his major position as playwright for the King's Men and the respect accorded him by his theatrical colleagues and their successors indicate at least a perception of innovative influence.

Fletcher learned early in his professional career not to buck the taste of the audience. After *The Faithful Shepherdess* his theatrical practices were with rather than against the tide. He was indeed a skilled professional and his talents in language and dramatic construction taught the dramatists who followed him. He was one of those intimately involved with the growth of the theater as an operating, commercial concern.

His productivity was great, but given the collaborative working conditions and the theatrical aims, perhaps not as remarkable to his time as it might seem to us. A contemporary writer for radio (in Britain) or television or films (in either the United States or Britain) could well have an equivalent production. The measure, of course, is quality. In measuring quality we return to the difficulty involved in the almost universal recognition that Fletcher was above all a wonderful deviser of scenes. His genius was truly for the theatrical moment.

His plots are the standard fare of the Renaissance stage. He read widely, kept up to date, and took and adapted to the stage whatever material seemed likely. Most of his characters are stock figures, but he created for the actors a wide range of stage roles from bizarre eccentrics to models of honor and high rhetoric. His rakehell wits directly appealed to his successors in the Restoration, and he did begin to create a group of witty heroines who would also be developed on the Restoration stage. Fletcher recognized the necessity of the intellectual, emotional, and spiritual equality of men and women to make one sort of comedy work, but he was also willing to forget those values for different comic effects. Fletcher's comic practice surely suggested and reached toward the comedy of manners; its achievement, however, was left to his successors.

In any summation something must be said of song, music, and sheer entertainment. In the tragedies and tragicomedies Fletcher always keeps the action intense. Build follows build, turn follows turn. The actors are always challenged by emotional peaks, and the action is consistently filled with variety and surprise. Comedies vary romance with farce and season, frequently, the whole with song. Fletcher's songs place him among the major lyricists of his day.

Fletcher's spoken verse is best when it is emphatic in one way or another. He gave his actors fine rhetorical pieces, serious or comic, to deliver. The power, especially in the serious pieces, is a consequence of Fletcher's greater sense of metrics than of imagery or metaphor. William Davenant found it appropriate to rewrite *Macbeth* by removing images and metaphors to make the language clearer. Fletcher's language has that sort of clarity. It is as difficult to recall Fletcherian images and metaphorical language as it is to recall the details of plot in his labyrinthine plays.

Yet the praise given his language is fully deserved. There is metrical vigor and a large range of surprising and effective vocabulary. His comic characters are, for the most part, witty; and when they are not, they are rowdy, often grotesque, and forceful. The praise given to his lyricism and his sentiment, however, is likely to escape the modern reader. Fletcher does not universalize as Shakespeare does. He remains almost entirely caught in the context of his own times.

In that sense he was one of the major baroque artists. We can admire the copiousness of his dramatic invention in character and scene and in that play of conceited wit, the sudden turns of thought and image that can transform the relations of appearance and reality. Fletcher's art and his achievement can be compared fruitfully with that of his younger French contemporary Jacques Callot (1592–1635). Callot's series of etchings—the *Caprices* (*Capricci di Varie Figure*), 1617–22—might well serve as illustrations to Fletcher's plays.

Callot's *Two Grotesque Musicians Dancing*, for example, conveys an extremity of human behavior and appearance congenial to Fletcher's own grotesques and eccentrics. *A Nobleman in Broad Cloak, Front View*, with its quick and loose lines, catches something both of grace and folly; the image is witty in the way that Fletcher's heroes and their high-flown language and scenes, gesture and countergesture, are witty. In *The Bandits Lair* we look out of a cave to dark figures fighting savagely at the cave's mouth. Outside a frilly, delicate tree contrasts sharply with the darkness of the cave's arched roof and the black figures in silhouetted combat; romance, violence, and fragility are contained in a briefly caught scene. This is the sort of witty and conceited image Fletcher could create and one of the effects he sought. It is not that the larger effects of a Rubens or Van Dyck, the monumental canvases of the great abstractions, War and Peace, Love and Lust, Honor and Shame were beyond his reach; but rather that his special genius and the focus of his practice and method of composition was for the part rather than the whole, the scene instead of the play.

In his own lifetime and for a number of years after, John Fletcher's dramatic reputation was enhanced by his association with Shakespeare and his succession to Shakespeare's position as writer in chief for the King's Men. In the long run he has suffered by constant comparison to his predecessor. To write in such close proximity and in brief instances collaboratively with overwhelming genius is hardly advantageous. Fletcher was a thorough professional, a master craftsman. He pleased the audiences of his day and for half a century beyond. He can still be read with pleasure and profit. Some few of his plays are still acted and more would be well worth reviving. These are not small achievements.

Notes and References

Chapter One

1. *Comedies and Tragedies Written by Francis Beaumont and John Fletcher Gentlemen* (London, 1647), A4v.
2. Quoted from *The Worthies of Kent* in *Shakespeare's Fellows*, by G. B. Harrison (London; John Lane, Bodley Head, 1923), 184–85.
3. John Aubrey, *Brief Lives*, ed. Oliver Lawson Dick (Ann Arbor: University of Michigan, 1957), 21.
4. E. K. Chambers, *The Elizabethan Stage* (Oxford: Oxford University Press, 1923), 3:216. Biographical details are drawn from Chambers and Charles Mills Gayley, *Beaumont, the Dramatist: A Portrait* (New York: Century, 1914) and G. E. Bentley, *The Jacobean and Caroline Stage*, vol. 3 (Oxford, 1956).
5. Quoted by Gayley, *Beaumont*, 43.
6. *The Complete Poetry of Ben Jonson*, ed. William B. Hunter, Jr. (New York: W. W. Norton & Co., 1963), 23.
7. *Ben Jonson*, ed. C. H. Herford and Percy Simpson (Oxford: Oxford University Press, 1925), 5:136.
8. The dates follow those in *The Later Jacobean and Caroline Dramatists: A Survey and Bibliography of Recent Studies in English Renaissance Studies*, ed. Terence P. Logan and Denzell S. Smith (Lincoln, Nebr. 1978). The date or dates between which the first production is likely will be given in parenthesis following the name of the play. For full discussion of dates and the question of collaboration the reader is referred to Logan and Smith, ed., *Later Jacobean and Caroline Dramatists;* E. K. Chambers, *The Elizabethan Stage*, vol. 3; G. E. Bentley, *Jacobean and Caroline Stage*, vol. 3; Cyrus Hoy, "The Shares of Fletcher and His Collaborators in the Beaumont and Fletcher Canon," *Studies in Bibliography* 8–9, 11–15 (1956–62); and Bertha Hensman, *The Shares of Fletcher, Field, and Massinger in Twelve Plays of the Beaumont and Fletcher Canon*, 2 vols. (Salzburg, 1974).
9. Antonia Fraser, *Mary Queen of Scots* (New York: Delacrote Press, 1969), 537, 540.
10. Bentley, *Jacobean and Caroline Stage*, 3:306.
11. Fuller, in Harrison, *Shakespeare's Fellows*, 184–85.
12. Gayley, *Beaumont*, 68.
13. Bentley, *Jacobean and Caroline Stage*, 3:307.
14. *English Literary Autographs 1550–1650*, ed. W. W. Greg (London: Oxford University Press, 1932), pt. 3, item 93.

15. Bentley, *Jacobean and Caroline Stage,* 3:307, quotes Shadwell and Dyce.

16. The boy companies and the distinctions between public and private theaters are discussed in Alfred Harbage, *Shakespeare and the Rival Traditions* (New York: MacMillan, 1952); Michael Shapiro, *Children of the Revels: The Boy Companies of Shakespeare's Time and Their Plays* (New York: Columbia University Press, 1977), and Andrew Gurr, *The Shakespearean Stage, 1574–1642* (Cambridge: Cambridge University Press, 1980).

17. *Hamlet,* ed. Harold Jenkins (London: Methuen, 1982), 2.2.337–42.

18. G. E. Bentley, *The Profession of Dramatist in Shakespeare's Time, 1590–1642* (Princeton: Princeton University Press, 1971), 37.

19. Ibid., 279.

20. Ibid., 125.

21. Ibid., 109.

22. Quoted in Bentley, *Jacobean and Caroline Stage,* 3:309.

23. Kenneth Muir, *Shakespeare as Collaborator* (London: Methuen, 1960), 147.

24. Aubrey, *Brief Lives,* 22.

Chapter Two

1. Shapiro, *Children of the Revels,* 105.

2. George Walton Williams in his edition of *The Woman Hater,* in *The Dramatic Works of the Beaumont and Fletcher Canon* (Cambridge, 1966), 1:151, concludes, "Fletcher's hand is to be found throughout III.i. 1–153, III.ii, IV.ii. 1–271, v.ii, iv" and "with less assurance in III.iii, IV.ii. 272–361, V.i." Beaumont, then, was the major contributor.

3. Alexander W. Upton, "Allusions to James I and His Court in Marston's *Fawn* and Beaumont's *Woman Hater,*" *Publications of the Modern Language Association* 44 (1929): 1048–65, argued for references to King James, the earl of Montgomery, Lord Hay, and others.

4. Chambers, *Elizabethan Stage,* 3:223.

5. Nancy Cotton Pearse, *John Fletcher's Chastity Plays* (Lewisburg, 1973), 195, 198.

6. 3.4.91–92; *Ben Jonson,* ed. Herford and Percy, vol. 5.

7. Translated by Allan H. Gilbert in *Literary Criticism: Plato to Dryden* (Detroit: Wayne State University Press, 1952), 511. Guarini's and Fletcher's views of tragicomedy are discussed by Arthur C. Kirsch, *Jacobean Dramatic Perspectives* (Charlottesville, 1972); Marvin T. Herrick, *Tragicomedy* (Urbana: University of Illinois Press, 1962); and Eugene M. Waith, *The Pattern of Tragicomedy in Beaumont and Fletcher* (New Haven, 1952).

8. Gilbert, *Literary Criticism,* 511.

9. Gurr, *Shakespearean Stage*, 212.

10. "Course words do but wound the ears; but a character of lewdness affronts the mind. If Cloe was meant to set off Clorin by contrast, Fletcher should have known that such weeds by juxtaposition do not set off but kill sweet flowers." Charles Lamb, *Specimens of the English Dramatic Poets* (New York: Johnson Reprint Company, 1970), 2:36. *Specimens* was first published in 1808, with notes added in 1818.

11. Florence Ada Kirk details the parallels in her edition of *The Faithful Shepherdess* (New York: Garland, 1980), 227.

12. *The Works of Beaumont and Fletcher* (London, 1908), 3:7.

13. James E. Savage, "The Date of Beaumont and Fletcher's *Cupid's Revenge*," *ELH* 15 (1948):286–94. Fredson Bowers edited the play in *Dramatic Works*, vol. 3, and following Cyrus Hoy assigns Fletcher 1.2.5, 2.3.4, 3.3.4, 4.2.4, and 5.2.4.

14. William W. Appleton, *Beaumont and Fletcher: A Critical Study* (London, 1956), takes the former position and Nancy Cotton Pearse, *John Fletcher's Chastity Plays*, the latter.

15. L. A. Beaurline, *The Dramatic Works*, 1:545, concludes that "Fletcher wrote the whole play for the early performances . . . or perhaps Beaumont collaborated on later scenes" and that subsequent transcription or a later revision removed most of the distinctive signs of Fletcher's hand.

16. Robert Ornstein, *The Moral Vision of Jacobean Tragedy* (Madison, 1965), 167.

17. John Donne, *The Satires, Epigrams and Verse Letters*, ed. W. Milgate (Oxford: Oxford University Press, 1967); "The Progresse of the Soule," lines 201–2.

18. Appleton, *Beaumont and Fletcher*, 50; Pearse's comments are in *Chastity Plays*, 199.

19. Baldwin Maxwell, *Studies in Beaumont, Fletcher, and Massinger* (New York: Octagon Books, 1969), makes the case for 1610 on the evidence of allusions. Hoy, "The Shares of Fletcher and His Collaborators," pt. 3, assigns Beaumont 1.1, 2.1, and 5.2, and Fletcher 1.2, 2.2–3, 3, 4, and 5.1, and 5.3–4.

20. M. C. Bradbrook, *The Growth and Structure of Elizabethan Comedy* (London: Chatto & Windus, 1962), 184.

Chapter Three

1. Kirsch, *Jacobean Dramatic Perspectives*, 3–4.

2. John F. Danby, *Elizabethan and Jacobean Poets* (London, n.d.), 180, first published as *Poets on Fortune's Hill* (London, 1952). Danby's argument is that the Fletcherian hero prefigures the Cavalier mentality.

3. Ornstein, *Moral Vision*, 164–65.

4. Philip Edwards, "The Danger Not the Death," in *Jacobean Theatre*, ed. John Russell Brown and Bernard Harris (London: Edward Arnold, 1960), 163. The quotation that follows is on 171.

5. Danby, *Elizabethan and Jacobean Poets*, 180.

6. *Coleridge on the Seventeenth Century*, ed. Roberta Florence Brinkley (Durham: Duke University Press, 1955), 655. Peter Davison, "The Serious Concerns of *Philaster*," *ELH* 30 (1963):1–15, argues against an escapist view of *Philaster* and for a sense of the play as seriously concerned with contemporary political affairs.

7. Harold S. Wilson, *"Philaster and Cymbeline,"* in *Shakespeare's Contemporaries*, ed. Max Bluestone and Norman Rabkin (Englewood Cliffs: Prentice-Hall, 1970), 340.

8. Philip J. Finkelpearl, "Beaumont, Fletcher, and 'Beaumont and Fletcher': Some Distinctions," *English Literary Renaissance* 1 (1971):155.

9. Arthur Mizener, "The High Design of *A King and No King*," *Modern Philology* 38 (1940):135.

10. Waith, *Pattern of Tragicomedy*, 86–98, 205–9.

11. Bentley, *Jacobean and Caroline Stage*, 3:356; Ian Fletcher, *Beaumont and Fletcher* (London, 1967), 60.

12. Waith, *Pattern of Tragicomedy*, 143. Denzell S. Smith, *Later Jacobean and Caroline Dramatists*, 42, cites the view of Ervin C. Brody that the play derives from contemporary histories and Lope de Vega's *El gran dugue de Moscovia*.

13. Pearse, *Chastity Plays*, 210. The quotation which follows is on 208.

14. Hensman, *Shares*, 1:71, 99. She attributes to Fletcher 2, 3.1, 3.4 and 4.2; 1 and 2 to Field; and 3.2–3, 4.1.2, and 4.4. to Massinger. She calls the play "a hurried collaboration . . . undertaken to provide an entertainment at which the Spanish and Venetian ambassadors were present in September 1618."

15. Eugene M. Waith, *Ideas of Greatness: Heroic Drama in England* (New York, 1971), 151.

16. Anthony Powell, *Hearing Secret Harmonies* (New York: Little, Brown, 1975), 144.

17. Aubrey, *Brief Lives*, 97–98.

18. Quoted from Pepys's *Diary* in Bentley, *Jacobean and Caroline Stage*, 3:345.

19. Ibid., 3:348.

Chapter Four

1. Marco Mincoff, "Fletcher's Early Tragedies," *Renaissance Drama* 7 (1968): 85. The succeeding quotation is on 91.

2. Leech, *The John Fletcher Plays* (London, 1962), 143.

3. Robert K. Turner in *Dramatic Works*, 2:3, follows Hoy's attribution in "The Shares of Fletcher."

4. H. Neville Davis, "Beaumont and Fletcher's *Hamlet*," in *Shakespeare, Man of the Theater*, ed. Kenneth Muir, Jay L. Halio, and D. J. Palmer (Newark: University of Delaware Press, 1983), 180.

5. In *Critical Essays of the Seventeenth Century*, ed. J. E. Spingarn, (Oxford: Oxford University Press, 1957), 190.

6. See *The Letters of John Chamberlain*, ed. Norman Egbert McClure (Philadelphia: American Philosophical Society, 1939), 424.

7. Ornstein, *Moral Vision*, 177.

8. Mincoff, "Fletcher's Early Tragedies," 72.

9. Ibid., 74.

10. The song is somewhat reminiscent both of Samuel Daniel's sonnet 49 in *Delia*, "Care-charmer sleep, son of the sable night," and Bartholomew Griffin's sonnet 15, "Care-charmer sleep, sweet ease in restless misery," in *Fidessa*.

11. D. J. Gordon, "Rubens and the Whitehall Ceiling," in *The Renaissance Imagination: Essays and Lectures by D. J. Gordon*, ed. Stephen Orgel (Berkeley: University of California Press, 1975), 35.

12. John Harold Wilson, *The Influence of Beaumont and Fletcher on Restoration Drama* (Columbus: Ohio State University Press, 1928), 45.

13. Paul D. Green, "Theme and Structure in Fletcher's *Bonduca*," *Studies in English Literature* 22, no. 2 (1982):305.

14. Quoted by Lawrence B. Wallis, *Fletcher, Beaumont and Company* (New York, 1947), 96. Swinburne was writing in the *English Review* 5 (1910).

15. Leech, *John Fletcher Plays*, 134.

16. J. D. Jump discusses sources, authorship, and stage history in his edition: *Rollo, Duke of Normandy* (Liverpool: Liverpool University Press, 1948). Bertha Hensman, *Shares of Fletcher*, credits Massinger with the passages Jump and others give to Jonson.

17. Quoted in Bentley, *Jacobean and Caroline Stage*, 3:415.

18. *The Tragedy of Sir John Van Olden Barnavelt*, ed. T. H. Howard-Hill (London: Malone Society, 1980), 13. Quotations are from this edition since the play was not printed in Glover and Waller.

19. Smith, Bentley, and Hensman all identify sources.

Chapter Five

1. The siege of Ostend took place in 1601–1603/4. Dudley Carleton in a letter of 15 January 1603/4 mentions the resupplying of Ostend (*Dudley Carleton to John Chamberlain, 1603–1624: Jacobean Letters*, ed.

Maurice Lee, Jr. (New Brunswick, N.J.: Rutgers University Press, 1972), 58. The reference to Ostend, a subject of conversation in 1604, may argue for the early date.

2. Bentley, *Jacobean and Caroline Stage,* 3:385.

3. Cyrus Hoy, "Fletcherian Romantic Comedy," *Research Opportunities in Renaissance Drama* 27 (1984):3.

4. The line caught Herman Melville's eye and he used it, varying "I" to "We," as an epigraph to "Barrington Isle and the Buccaneers" (in *The Encantadas*).

5. Hans Walter Gabler in his introduction to the play in *The Dramatic Works,* 4:417, argues that both *The Little Thief* and *Monsieur Thomas* were written for the Children. Hensman, *Shares of Fletcher,* 2:391, dates the former ca. 1614 and the latter 1615.

6. *Coleridge on the Seventeenth Century,* 671.

7. Appleton, *Beaumont and Fletcher,* 74.

8. Bentley, *Jacobean and Caroline Stage,* 3:427. Publication and production history is also discussed in the introduction of Rota Herzberg Lister's *A Critical Edition of John Fletcher's The Wild Goose Chase* (New York: Garland, 1980).

9. Quoted in Bentley, *Jacobean and Caroline Stage,* 3:427.

10. Leech, *John Fletcher Plays,* 76.

11. A probable reference to Ben Jonson's *The Devil is an Ass* (1616) makes 1617 a likely date, but the play has been dated as late as 1625, the year of Fletcher's death. Bentley, *Jacobean and Caroline Stage,* 3:322, opts for the 1617 date and Hensman, *Shares of Fletcher* 1:22, for 1625.

12. Quoted in Bentley, *Jacobean and Caroline Stage,* 3:320.

13. Quoted by George Walton Williams in his introduction to *The Chances* (in *The Dramatic Works,* vol. 4).

14. Bentley, *Jacobean and Caroline Stage,* 3:364. George Walton Williams in *The Dramatic Works,* 3:3–11, also discusses the play's history.

15. *Coleridge on the Seventeenth Century,* 672.

16. Quoted in Bentley, *Jacobean and Caroline Stage,* 3:328. The information concerning Herbert's takings from *The Custom of the Country* are found in the same place. The quotation from Pepys's *Diary* is from Bentley (ibid., 3:325).

Chapter Six

1. *Essays of John Dryden,* ed. W. P. Ker (New York: Russell & Russell, 1961), 1:81.

2. Quoted in Wilson, *Influence of Beaumont and Fletcher,* 15.

3. Quoted in Wallis, *Fletcher, Beaumont and Company,* 55.

4. Ibid., 247.

5. Ibid.

6. *Coleridge on the Seventeenth Century*, 656, 658–59.

7. Ibid., 671–72.

8. Algernon Charles Swinburne, *Studies in Prose and Poetry* (London: Chatto & Windus, 1894), 71.

9. *The Cambridge History of English Literature* (London: Cambridge University Press, 1910), 6:124–25.

10. *A Literary History of England*, ed. Albert C. Baugh (New York: Appleton-Century Crofts, 1948), 575–76.

11. Ornstein, *Moral Vision*, 163.

Selected Bibliography

PRIMARY SOURCES

Comedies and Tragedies Written by Francis Beaumont and John Fletcher Gentlemen. London: Humphrey Robinson & Humphrey Moseley, 1647.

Fifty Comedies and Tragedies. London: John Martyn, Henry Herringman, & Richard Marriot, 1679.

The Works of Beaumont and Fletcher. Edited by Alexander Dyce. 11 vols. London: Edward Moxon, 1843–46.

The Works of Beaumont and Fletcher Varioroum Edition. Edited by A. H. Bullen et al. 4 vols. London: G. Bell & Sons and A. H. Bullen, 1904–12.

The Works of Francis Beaumont and John Fletcher. Edited by Arnold Glover and A. R. Waller. 10 vols. Cambridge: Cambridge University Press, 1905–12.

The Dramatic Works in the Beaumont and Fletcher Canon. Edited by Fredson Bowers et al. 6 vols. Cambridge: Cambridge University Press, 1966–.

SECONDARY SOURCES

Appleton, William W. *Beaumont and Fletcher: A Critical Study*. London: Allen & Unwin, 1956. Still a useful survey, but to be supplemented with later works.

Bentley, Gerald Eades. *The Jacobean and Caroline Stage*. 7 vols. Oxford: Oxford University Press, 1940–68. A compendium of information basic to the study of Jacobean and Caroline drama.

————. *The Profession of Dramatist in Shakespeare's Time, 1590–1642*. Princeton: Princeton University Press, 1971. A study of the working conditions of the dramatist. Helpful for placing Fletcher in his professional context.

Danby, John. *Elizabethan and Jacobean Poets*. London: Faber & Faber, 1964. Contains two stimulating chapters on Beaumont and Fletcher, locating them in the Sidneian tradition and as forerunners of the age to come.

Edwards, Philip. "The Danger not the Death: the Art of John Fletcher." In *Stratford-upon-Avon Studies*, Vol. 1. Edited by John Russell Brown and Bernard Harris. London: Edward Arnold, 1960. A perceptive study of Fletcher's tragicomic style.

Ellis-Fermor, Una. *The Jacobean Drama.* London: Methuen, 1936. Contains a useful essay on Beaumont and Fletcher as well as presenting an overview of Jacobean drama.

Frost, David. *The School of Shakespeare.* Cambridge: Cambridge University Press, 1968. Devotes a chapter to Shakespeare's influence on the "Beaumont and Fletcher" plays.

Finkelpearl, Philip J. "Beaumont, Fletcher, and 'Beaumont & Fletcher': Some Distinctions." *English Literary Renaissance* 1 (1971): 144–64. Argues for a distinction between the early plays of "Beaumont and Fletcher" and the later works.

Hensman, Bertha. *The Shares of Fletcher, Field, and Massinger in Twelve Plays of the Beaumont and Fletcher Canon.* 2 vols. Salzburg: Institut für Englishe Sprache und Literatur, 1974. Useful analysis of collaboration and sources.

Hoy, Cyrus. "The Shares of Fletcher and His Collaborators in the Beaumont and Fletcher Cannon." *Studies in Bibliography* 8–12 (1956–62). Basic study for the question of colloboration and attribution.

Kirsch, Arthur C. "*Cymbeline* and Coterie Dramaturgy." *English Literary History* 34 (1967):285–306. Important study of the relation of Fletcher to Shakespearean romance and coterie theaters.

———. *Jacobean Dramatic Perspectives.* Charlottesville: University Press of Virginia, 1972. A helpful discussion of Jacobean drama with chapters on Guarini and Jonson and Beaumont and Fletcher.

Leech, Clifford. *The John Fletcher Plays.* London: Chatto & Windus, 1962. An excellent examination of the major plays.

Logan, Terence P., and **Smith, Denzell S.** *The Later Jacobean and Caroline Dramatists: A Survey and Bibliography of Recent Studies in English Renaissance Studies.* Lincoln: University of Nebraska Press, 1978. An invaluable annotated bibliography.

Mincoff, Marco. "Fletcher's Early Tragedies." *Renaissance Drama* 7 (1964):70–94. Argues for Fletcher's neoclassicism.

Mizener, Arthur. "The High Design of *A King and No King.*" *Modern Philology* 38 (1941):133–54. A major discussion of the play.

Ornstein, Robert. *The Moral Vision of Jacobean Tragedy.* Madison: University of Wisconsin Press, 1965. Presents a stimulating negative view of Fletcher.

Pearse, Nancy Cotton. *John Fletcher's Chastity Plays: Mirrors of Modesty.* Lewisburg: Bucknell University Press, 1973. Useful discussion of plays from the perspective of sexual themes and attitudes.

Potter, Lois, et al. *The Revels History of Drama in English.* Vol. 4. London: Methuen, 1981. A valuable survey of theatrical conditions, actors, playwrights, and plays.

Waith, Eugene M. *Ideas of Greatness: Heroic Drama in England.* New York: Barnes & Noble, 1971. Especially useful for its examination of Fletcher's characterization.

————. *The Pattern of Tragicomedy in Beaumont and Fletcher.* New Haven: Yale University Press, 1952. Basic to any study of Fletcher.

Wallis, Lawrence. *Fletcher, Beaumont and Company: Entertainers to the Jacobean Gentry.* 1947. Reprint. New York: Octagon Books, 1968. Dated, but contains a helpful discussion of the reputation of the plays.

Index